Travels in Burgundy

Chalon-sur-Saône, St Vincent Cathedral

Travels in Burgundy

Mary Elsy
with
Jill Norman

MEREHURST PRESS
LONDON

Published 1989 by Merehurst Press
Ferry House, 51-57 Lacy Road,
Putney, London SW15 1PR

Co-Published in Australia and New Zealand by
Child and Associates
5 Skyline Place, French's Forest
Sydney 2086
Australia

ISBN 1 85391 041 4

Designed and produced by Snap! Books

Printed in Great Britain by Butler and Tanner Ltd,
Frome, Somerset

Typeset by Maggie Spooner Typesetting
Illustrations by Ann Johns
Maps by Sue Lawes
Cover illustration: Watercolour by William
McEvoy, 1884, by kind permission of Sebastian
d'Orsai Ltd, 39 Theobalds Road, London WC1.

Contents

Travels in Burgundy

Author's Preface

Although Burgundy lacks a sea coast, it is one of the best parts of France to visit for a short stay and/or a quiet holiday. Except for its motorways and towns like Dijon and Beaune, it is seldom overcrowded. It is said that the Gods have blessed the Burgundians with three gifts — wine, art and archaeology. Add to these a varied and colourful countryside, old abbeys, churches and châteaux, restful waterways, tranquil old towns and villages and one of the best tables in France.

The central part of *Travels in Burgundy* provides a plan for a 14 days' tour of Burgundy, beginning at Châtillon-sur-Seine. From here, you visit the abbey of Fontenay to see how life was lived in a Cistercian abbey, then Montbard, home of the Comte de Buffon, France's greatest naturalist, and Mont Auxois, where the patriot Vercingétorix was finally defeated by Julius Caesar, and, if time, the fantastically-decorated home of that unfortunate clown, Bussy-Rabutin and the old fortified town of Flavigny. From Semur, you take the main motorway to sleepy old Dijon, city of museums and churches. Next comes Burgundy's wine regions where you will have the strange feeling that you are moving down a magnified and very expensive wine list. From Beaune, the wine capital, you will continue southwards to Tournus with its delightful old houses and cobbled streets. from Mâcon, you will drive westwards to Cluny, an abbey once so large and strong, that it was a powerful state on its own. Other towns to visit are Charolles and Paray-le-Monial before departing for a brief look at Burgundy's industrial area and the old towns of Autun and Saulieu on the Morvan's eastern edge. The Morvan is an area to meander through slowly, staying at Château-Chinon and maybe St Honoré-les-Bains. Nevers, Charité-sur-Loire and Clamecy come before Vézelay on its hill. More old towns follow, such as Auxerre, Avallon, and Sens; also celebrated and sumptuous châteaux, such as Tanlay and Ancy-le-Franc before your holiday ends.

The itinerary provides a basic route for each day and, for those with time available, offers suggestions for additional trips marked in the text as *Detours*.

To give added interest to your journey the following section offers background information on aspects of the region — most particularly its cuisine. The final section gives some samples of menus and recipes of the region's most typical dishes.

Introduction
to
Burgundy

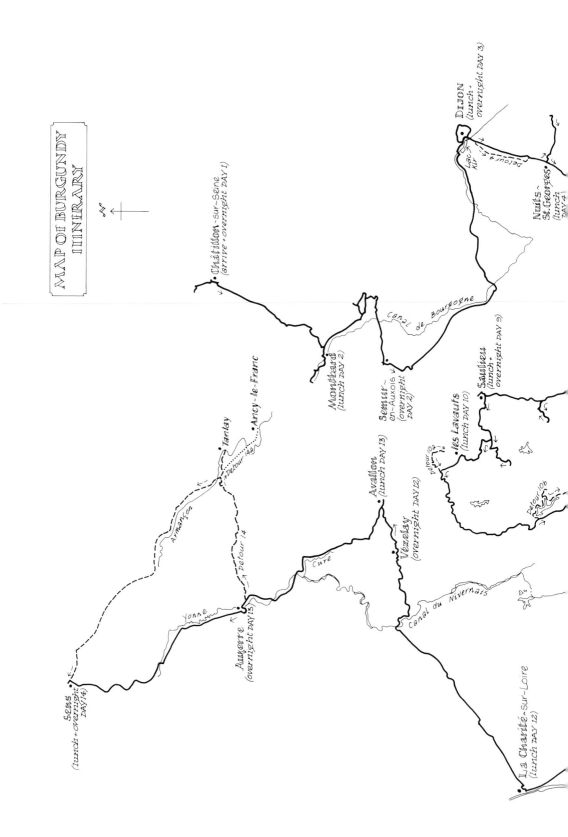

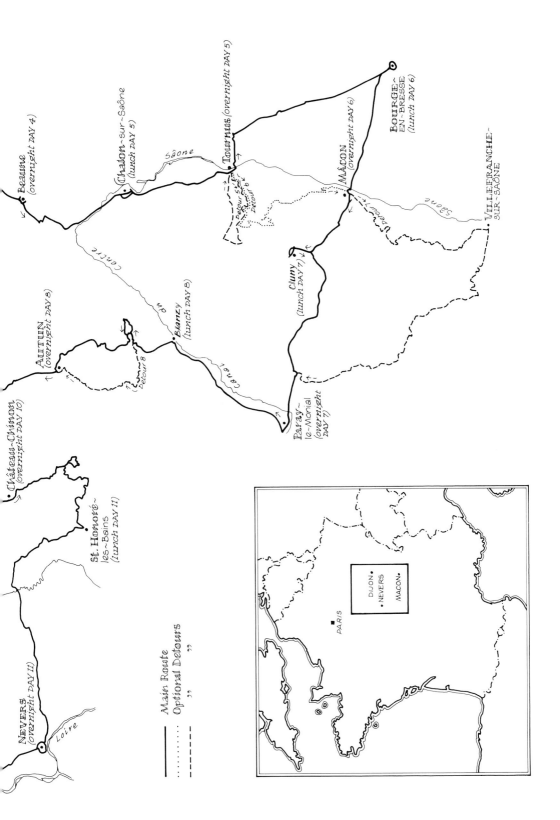

Beaune (overnight DAY 4)

Chalon~sur~Saône (lunch DAY 5)

Saône

Tournus (overnight DAY 5)

Mâcon (overnight DAY 6)

Bourge~ en~Bresse (lunch DAY 6)

Villefranche~ sur~Saône

Centre

Detour 5

Detour 6

Saône

Linou

Detour

Autun (overnight DAY 8)

d'n

Blanzy (lunch DAY 8)

Cluny (lunch DAY 7)

Detour 8

Paray~ le~Monial (overnight DAY 7)

Château~Chinon (overnight DAY 10)

St. Honoré~ les~Bains (lunch DAY 11)

Nevers (overnight DAY 11)

Loire

Main Route
Optional Detours
"   "

PARIS

DIJON•
•NEVERS
MACON•

The Morvan

Land Use and Agriculture

Burgundy, roughly wedged between the Loire and the Saône rivers, with Sens at its northwest extremity and Mâcon in the southeast, is more of a historical than a clearly-defined geographical region. It is a collection of districts, such as the Senonais, the Gatinais, the Puisaye, the Nivernais, the Auxois, the Charollais, etc., with each region having its own attractions. Its formation and position, linking north and south, have made it a transitional area, a crossroads of France, and a meeting place of Atlantic and Mediterranean influences.

The countryside is remarkably varied with contrastingly-coloured patchworks of fields, hills and valleys, grassy plateaux and thick woods, canals, rivers and streams, and even its own rocky mountain region, the Morvan. To the east lies the plain of the Saône valley, to the north, the plateaux of Lower Burgundy: southwards are the Mâconnais and Beaujolais uplands and the Charolles hills; westwards the wooded rugged Morvan. At its heart and spread over the limestone plateaux of upper Burgundy, is the Côte d'Or, with some of the world's most celebrated vineyards.

Burgundy's main rivers, the Loire, Saône, Yonne, and Seille and their tributaries and canals make up about 1200 kms of navigable waterways. In fact, a peaceful waterborne pace is as good a way as any of savouring its territory. Several British companies organise cruising holidays in Burgundy. Or, you could write direct to France. (Bourgogne Voies Navigables, 1-2 quai de la République, 89000 Auxerre, France. Tel: 86.52.18.99.)

Burgundy is one of France's wealthiest and most productive regions. Activities here range from extensive vine cultivation, rearing famous breeds of cattle, such as the Charolais, agriculture and food industries to timber forestry, stone-quarrying, coal-mining (around Le Creusot, a centre of steel-working and heavy industry), ceramics and some uranium-prospecting.

Burgundy has a continental climate. Winter is crisp and cold. Summer can be very hot but with occasional refreshing showers. The best time to come is in May, or in September and October for vine-harvesting and wine festivals.

History

Bones found at Solutré near Mâcon — a site at the foot of a superb limestone escarpment which has given its name to a prehistoric culture — are proof that people lived in this region ten to thirty thousand years before Christ.

The Celtic Edueni, Lingoni and Sequani invaded the region during the 6th century BC. The Saône valley became an important trade route down which tin, mined in Cornwall, could be taken to Marseilles and sent by sea to Mediterranean countries.

By the first century BC the region was divided up between several Celtic tribes. It was at Mont Beuvray in Burgundy that the unity of the Gallic tribes was achieved, and at Alise-Ste-Reine that the defeat of the Gallic leader, Vercingétorix, took place in 52 BC, and Gaul lost its independence to the Romans.

The Burgondes, a Scandinavian people, emigrated from the Baltic coast in the 1st century AD to settle in south Germany. Worms was their capital: their chief clan was the Nibelungs. Although Romanised, their drive westwards resulted in their massacre by the Romans, allied with the Huns, as is recounted in the famous epic, the *Nibelungeleid*. The remaining Burgundians were allocated land around Lake Geneva, but gradually fanned out towards the Saône and Rhône valleys. These tall fair people, warlike, intelligent and well-led, merged with the tribes already settled there. In 534 their kingdom was taken over by the powerful Merovingian Franks, led by Clovis, but it remained intact and eventually expanded to include even Arles in Provence: later Carolingian Franks imposed a heavy grip on the realm.

When Charlemagne's empire was divided in three in 843, most of the Burgundian kingdom became part of Lotharingia, which stretched from the Mediterranean to the North Sea. Later the part west of the Saône, the nucleus of the future Burgundy, went to the Frankish king, Charles the Bald. In spite of continuing struggles with Franks, Magyars, Moor and Normans, the realm evolved into a rich independent duchy, linked by blood with the royal house of France.

During the turmoil of the Dark Ages, many monks, seeking refuge from Norman invaders, had settled in Burgundy, and the church became a powerful force during the religious revival that followed. Burgundy was one of the most important bastions of Christianity; its prestige even limiting the powers of the dukes, although they were pleased to bask in the reflected glory it brought their duchy. The monks were prolific builders and the presence of so much good stone in the region enabled them to erect innumerable grandiose abbeys, churches and cathedrals. In no other part of France is there greater evidence of the immense power and wealth of the medieval church.

When the young duke, Philip de Rouvres, died heirless, aged 17, in 1361, the duchy reverted to the French crown. John the Good (King of France) presented it to his fourth son, Philip the Bold. In 1364, this Valois was created Duke of Burgundy and became the first of its four great dukes. At its height, their 'little' empire comprised the Low Countries, the Franche Comté, Picardy, Artois, Luxembourg, the counties of Charollais, Nevers, Thionville and Revel, also Lower Lorraine and Upper Alsace, as well as ducal Burgundy.

Philip, shrewd and far-seeing, considerably added to his domain by diplomacy and the advantageous marriages of his daughters. To prevent the English from obtaining Flanders, Charles V, (the next French king) had helped his younger brother to marry Margaret, its heiress. Philip subdued the rebellious Flemish cities and came to terms with the people, also with England, whose wool was needed for their cloth industry. Philip was a great patron of the arts. He owned a magnificent library, and all his possessions — furniture, plate and jewels — were exquisite. Perhaps it's not too surprising that he died in debt.

His son, John the Fearless (r.1404-1419), coarse, brave, wily, more Flemish than French, inherited many difficulties. He soon found himself at odds with Louis, Duke of Orléans, brother of the mad Charles VI (France's next king). Louis's subsequent murder by John's men in Paris resulted in an even more turbulent and divided France. As the Orléans' faction was led by Louis's uncle, Bernard d'Armagnac, the feud was always referred to as one between Burgundians and Armagnacs.

In 1419, John himself was murdered at a meeting with the new French dauphin, who was under Armagnac influence, on the Yonne bridge at Montereau, and his son, Philip the Good (r.1419-1467) came to power in Burgundy.

Philip, obliged to avenge his father's death, aided the English during the last stages of the Hundred Years' War. It was he who had Joan of Arc sold to the English for 10,000 ecus d'or. However, with the Treaty of Arras (1435), Philip made his peace with the French crown.

The greatest of the four dukes, he was known as the Grand Duc d'Occident, and became almost a king himself. His court was one of the most magnificent in Europe. Kings and emperors were proud to be members of his select Order of the Golden Fleece. He had his own coins minted, his own States General. When he dies, he had practically freed his duchy from French control.

Although Charles the Bold (r.1467-1477) — more often called 'the Rash' — wanted to expand his domain even more, and perhaps revive the old kingdom of Lotharingia, his inheritance was too diverse to make this possible. His wars were unpopular; his army too small.

After Charles' death, hewn down by Swiss pikemen when fighting against Duke René in Lorraine, wily King Louis XI seized a large part of his duchy for the crown. In Dijon, the dukes' capital, the Palais des Ducs became the Logis du Roi. The province was placed under the authority of a governor. It was not until 1789 that the whole of Burgundy was officially made part of France and divided into the approximate departments of Yonne, Côte d'Or, the Saône et Loire and Nièvre. On the whole the Revolution was welcomed in Burgundy but was less bloody than in other parts of France.

The First World War left Burgundy unharmed and, fortunately, it did not suffer as much damage as other places during the Second.

Famous People

Up to and during the Middle Ages, Burgundian intellectual life centred around the churches and monasteries, first chiefly the Abbey St Germain d'Auxerre, then the abbey of Cluny. The influential St Bernard (1091-1153) born at Fontaine-les-Dijon, and the founder of the abbey at Clairvaux, left behind some remarkable letters and theological treatises. The 12th century was a period of chivalry and gave rise to the *Chanson des Gestes* (poems of heroic and legendary exploits). Mystery and passion were a popular form of theatre. In the 15th century, the powerful Dukes of Burgundy encouraged the chroniclers to write about — and embellish — their reigns.

Among the humanist philosophers of the 16th century were Pontus de Thyard (1521-1605), a Mâconnais, and Theodore de Bèze (1519-1605) from Vézelay. Bonaventure des Périers (1510-1544), a classicist from Arnay-le-Duc, published *Cymbalum Mundi* in 1538 (it purported to be a translation from the classics). The text, which was composed of four satirical dialogues directed against the Christian faith, liturgy and discipline, was suppressed. He also wrote some graceful verses.

17th-century Burgundy was dominated by the great figure of Dijonnais Jacques Bénigne de Bossuet (1627-1704), a stout defender of the Catholic faith and a cultured humanist and theologian, particularly renowned for his sermons and funeral orations. He had some influence on Madame de Sévigné, a cousin of the rascally Comte de Bussy-Rabutin (1618-93). The publication of Bussy-Rabutin's *Histoire Amoureuse des Gaules* in 1655, which contained some scandalous anecdotes about various ladies of the court (even the virtuous Madame de Sévigné was not omitted) earned him a term in the Bastille.

Another 17th-century man who should perhaps be included is France's famous military engineer, Seigneur de Vauban (1633-1707) from St Léger Vauban. At the end of his life he published *Project d'une dîme royale*, which advocated equality of taxation and so caused much royal displeasure.

Two other 17th-century writers are Prosper Crébillon, the elder, (1674-1762) born at Dijon, a dramatist chiefly of tragic melodramas; and Alexis Piron (1689-1773) also from Dijon, a light and witty poet and dramatist. The naturalist, the Comte de Buffon (1707-88), who was born at the château de Montbard, divided his life between the administration of his estate and his work. His 15-volume *Histoire Naturelle* (published between 1749 and 1767) made him one of the founders of modern natural history.

Rather different was the novelist, Nicholas Restif de la Bretonne (1734-1806) from Sacy, the son of a peasant. His writing, although prolific, does not possess much literary merit, but gives a good picture of how ordinary people lived then.

Nearer to our time is Alphonse Lamartine (1790-1869), one of the four great poets of the Romantic movement. Lamartine extols the beauty of his home at St Point-de-Milly in his *Meditations*. A romantic of rather a different kind was the internationally acclaimed writer Sidonie Gabrielle Colette (1873-1954), born and brought up at Saint-Sauveur in Puisaye. She depicts her mother and background in *Sido*.

Novelist Jules Renard (1864-1910) who came from the craggy wooded Morvan was a realist with a wry sense of humour who excelled in depicting village characters, also animals. Very different again was internationalist Romain Rolland (1868-1944) from Clamecy, an idealist, biographer and philosopher. He was an anti-rationalist, an opponent of catholicism and nationalism and had a mystical belief in humanity. His ten volumes' novel *Jean Christophe* was an extension of his biographies, but on an imaginative plain.

Burgundy, because of its crossroads position, has long been a focus of art. During the 15th century, its great dukes encouraged many artists from Paris and Flanders to settle in Dijon, which became one of the art centres of Europe. Sculptors Claus Sluter (d. c. 1405) and his nephew Claus de Werve (d. c. 1439) spent most of their lives in Dijon.

From the north came artists Jean Malouel (d. 1415), uncle of the Limbourgs, Jean de Beaumetz (d. 1396) and Henri Bellechose (c. 1380-1443) who created a Flemish Burgundian style noted for its precision and richness of colour. Amongst the celebrated works produced then were the polyptych at Beaune's Hôtel Dieu, by Roger van der Weyden (1399-1464). Frescoes came back into fashion especially in churches. The works of Dijonnais, Pierre Spicre (d. 1478), may be seen in Notre Dame at Beaune. He also designed the pictures for the tapestries in Notre-Dame and Hôtel Dieu.

During the 16th century, Burgundy came under the influence of Italy and the classical style of the Renaissance. However, the reunion with France tended to make the province less artistically independent. Paris and Versailles set the style. Sculptor Jean Dubois (1626-94) in the 17th and Bouchardon (1698-1762) and Attiret (1728-1804) in the 18th century had a great influence on their time. The same may be said of François Devosge (1732-1811) and Jean Baptiste Greuze (1725-1805), a very dramatic artist.

Pierre Paul Prudhon (1758-1823), a pupil of Devosge, who began in obscurity and died in misery, knew a period of success when official painter to two empresses, Josephine and Marie Louise. His work continued the loose, melting, mysterious manner favoured by Greuze, and was a forerunner of Romanticism.

François Rude (1784-1855) from Dijon was another pupil of Devosge. Other Dijonnais were artists J.F.G. Colson (1733-1803) and Claude Hoin (1750-1817); sculptor Claude Ramey (1751-1838) and engraver Alphonse Legros (1837-1911). Nearer our time is animal sculptor François Pompon. And perhaps I should also mention that great artist in steel, Gustave Eiffel (1832-1923), was also born at Dijon. Neither should one forget that Burgundian, Nicéphore Niepce, who had the honour of producing the first photograph in 1822.

Hôtel-Dieu, Beaune

The Epicure's Guide

You will eat well in Burgundy. The food of the province is plentiful and good; Charolais beef, chickens from Bresse, freshwater fish, snails, Morvan hams, grains, vegetables and soft fruits, cow's and goat's milk cheeses all contribute to the robust cuisine bourgeoise that is typically Burgundian. And of course there is a Burgundy wine to go with virtually every dish.

Burgundy is not a geographical entity, it is made up of several different regions; its past under the Dukes of Burgundy is what made it a united province. In the north and west is the beautiful, rolling countryside that you reach in just over an hour's drive from Paris, to the east the plain of the Saône, in the middle the calcareous plateau of the Côte where the greatest red and white burgundies are grown, and to the south the forested granite mass of the Morvan and the Mâconnais and Beaujolais hills.

There is nothing new about cuisine du terroir in Burgundy; because the region is so varied, agriculture is diverse and local ingredients have always been important. Auxerre is renowned for its cherries, the Saône valley for vegetables; red and black currants, raspberries and strawberries are cultivated among the vineyards of the Hautes-Côtes. In addition to pig rearing the Morvan provides game from the forests and crayfish and trout from its many streams, while bigger fish are caught in the Saône and the Loire. The Burgundians are hearty eaters — gourmands as well as gourmets — and of course no meal is complete without its accompanying bottle or bottles of grand or simple wine, according to the dish and the occasion.

Wine is widely used in cooking too — coq au vin, boeuf à la bourguignonne, ouefs en meurette, pochouse bourguignonne, jambon persillé, civet de porc, haricots au vin rouge are staples of the Burgundian table.

For thousands of years people have passed through Burgundy and left their traces. The first vines were probably planted about 600 BC, brought from the Greek settlement at Marseilles. In the Middle Ages the powerful monasteries of Cluny and Cîteaux owned large vineyards, including some of today's most prestigious appellations. The austere Cistercian order, in particular, did much to promote good vine husbandry and the fame of the local wines; indeed they founded the Clos de Vougeot, whose cellars so impressed Rabelais.

Under the Valois dukes (14th- to 15th-century) Burgundy encompassed Flanders, Luxembourg and parts of France; Dijon, the capital of the dukes, was the vibrant centre of feudal Europe. Known as 'lords of the best wines of Christendom', they set high standards for both wine and food. In the ducal palace you can still see the great kitchens where fires once burned beneath six open chimneys to prepare banquets for the dukes and their guests. It is from this time too that the Low Countries acquired their taste for burgundy, rather as the English became bordeaux enthusiasts for similar historical reasons.

Dijon is still the gastronomic centre of Burgundy. Each year at the beginning of November the Dijon Food Fair takes place and for two weeks the town is crowded with people tasting foods and wines from all over France. If you are in the region in November it is certainly worth a visit.

Dijon's claim to international fame is of course mustard. Moutarde de Dijon refers to the style of mustard — a pungent, creamy mustard, first made here by mixing finely ground mustard seeds with verjuice. It can legally be made anywhere in the world, but Dijon remains the mustard capital of France, producing about 80 per cent of the country's output. Today wine or vinegar may be used instead of verjuice, and the best mustard seeds are imported from Canada, not picked from the local fields. Mustard made with coarsely ground seeds, called moutarde à l'ancienne is always milder. Flavoured mustards such as tarragon, fines herbes, lime or four fruit mustard are fashionable again, though there are less varieties than in the eighteenth and nineteenth centuries when mustard was at the height of its popularity. In those days mustard was bought fresh daily from special mustard shops; you can still buy it from the attractive Grey-Poupon shop which is full of colourful hand-painted mustard jars of all sizes.

Mustard finds its way into many local dishes. Andouillettes and andouilles (chitterling sausages) renowned in Chablis, Clamecy and Mâcon as well as Dijon often include it in the recipe. Sausages are very popular; look out for air-dried rosette du Morvan and the many fresh or smoked sausages served hot, often with a potato purée. One of the great Burgundian dishes, served traditionally at Easter, is jambon persillé. The ham is simmered with pig's trotters and white wine, then the meat is cut into chunks, put in a bowl and the cooking liquor mixed with parsley poured over it and chilled until it sets. Ham is also served hot, usually braised and served with a spicy cream sauce. This dish, called saupiquet des Amognes, is a very old speciality of the Morvan and Nivernais.

You will find snails everywhere in Burgundy, carved in stone on ancient buildings, on restaurant linen, as emblems over shops. The large Burgundy snail, *helix pomatia*, was once gathered in the vineyards, but now they are fast disappearing with the increased use of agricultural chemicals. Today's snails are reared and packed in cans and are probably imported. Mâcon is reckoned to have the best snails served in the usual way with garlic, shallot and parsley butter. Further north, at Sens, they use snails to stuff mushrooms.

Mention meat, poultry, or game in Burgundy and it usually suggests a rich wine or wine and cream sauce. A garnish of mushrooms, small glazed onions and cubes of salt pork is a sign of a Burgundian dish anywhere. You will find it in boeuf à la bourguignonne and in coq au vin, or coq au Chambertin as you may see on local menus, though I wonder whether anyone puts a bottle of Chambertin in the cooking pot these days. Chicken in a white wine sauce might be listed as poulet au Meursault. Chicken sautéd with a wine vinegar sauce, chicken with crayfish, chicken or small game birds with grapes, rabbit or veal with mustard, pork or wild boar with chestnuts and wild mushrooms — all combine local ingredients to provide a sumptuous choice on the table.

The best chickens of the region are from Bresse to the east of the Côte d'Or. Protected by an appellation since 1957, they are handsome white birds with blue feet, reared on maize and skim milk. They must be free ranging on grass and farmers are only allowed to raise 500 at a time. They certainly have more flavour than other chickens, but then they cost three times as much. If you visit a market you may still find someone there selling live chickens; a poulet de Bresse has an identification tag around the left leg.

Wine, cream, onions, mushrooms and garlic all crop up again in fish cooking. One of the most famous dishes is pochouse, a fish stew for which the essentials are a mixture of freshwater fish, including eel, bacon or salt pork, white wine, onion and garlic, with croûtons to garnish. Meurette, a red wine sauce, is one of the cornerstones of Burgundian cooking. It is used primarily for fish dishes, and is particularly good with carp, perch and eel. The same sauce is also served with eggs; oeufs en meurette are poached eggs in a red wine sauce garnished with fried croûtons.

Salmon from the Loire is plentiful, sometimes prepared with the mint that grows wild along the banks. Trout in wine and cream sauce, pike and trout mousses, écrevisses à la nage — crayfish in an aromatic broth of wine and herbs, and burbot, called lotte de rivière, are other specialities worth trying.

Unlike some regions, Burgundy is rich in vegetable dishes, many of them very old. They are usually intended to accompany a meat or fish dish, not to be the main course of a meal. Chestnuts and onions in red wine accompany wild boar or pork in the Morvan; cabbage is baked or stuffed with apple and sausages; beans are stewed in wine and spices, potatoes turn up in gratins, sautéd with onions, as potato cakes or pancakes, often with cubes of salt pork. Crosnes, or Chinese artichokes, are a delicious curiosity grown in the region since the early years of the century. They are small pearly tubers, rather shell-like in appearance, best sautéd in butter or served in a light cream sauce. All sorts of cultivated and wild mushrooms are used, sautéd with shallots, slow cooked with diced ham, garlic and parsley, or marinated in walnut oil and herbs. Robust green salads with bacon and croûtons or ham and herbs occur on most menus; in winter there are warm lentil or cabbage salads and occasionally a lovely salad of green beans and truffles.

Burgundy makes a lot of cheeses, but with the exception of Epoisses, they do not have a reputation beyond the region. Epoisses, named after a village, is a small round cow's milk cheese with an orange-red rind that is regularly washed with marc, a smooth, butter-coloured paste and a pronounced flavour and bouquet. Other cheeses worth trying are Montrachet and Vézelay, both cylindrical goat's milk cheeses often wrapped in vine or chestnut leaves; Lormes, another goat cheese shaped like a truncated cone and with a pronounced flavour; Cîteaux, a rich, unaggressive cow's milk cheese made by the Trappist monks; Pierre-qui-Vire, another monastic cheese also made from cow's milk and with a penetrating smell, St-Florentin and Soumaintrain, cow's milk cheeses with a washed rind tang and a fine texture.

In *Prisons et Paradis* Colette recalls her childhood in Burgundy and how plentiful cheese was: 'There was no phase in the cheese's life from which we did not derive advantage; the quivering, scarcely set jelly, then the big pressed masses of curd, cooked in thick layers on great, salted, open tart crusts. Then the finished cheese, generally hewn out in triangles, firmly held on to its slice of bread beneath the field's worker's thumb . . . To follow, a dandelion salad bathed in walnut oil, a glass of wine . . .

'Not far from my village there were farms where they made Soumaintrains, and the red Saint-Florentins, which came to our market decked out in beetroot leaves. And I remember how the butter alone had the right to wear the long, the elegant chestnut leaf, delicately toothed along the edges . . .'

For one of its cheese dishes, la gougère, Burgundy uses gruyère from the mountains to the east. It is choux pastry studded with cubes of cheese, made either as a large ring to replace the cheese course or in small puffs to serve with aperitifs. Sens and Tonnerre are particularly known for their gougères.

As you drive through northern Burgundy you will not be able to miss the fields of wheat and other grains, so it will come as no surprise that Burgundy is noted for breads and pastries. The local walnut bread is one of my favourites; and there are breads flavoured with spicy seeds such as cumin, sesame and aniseed. Dijon is renowned for nonnettes and pain d'épice, or spice bread, made with flour, yeast, honey and a touch of anise. It may include nuts or fruit, be coated with sugar or chocolate and comes in every shape you can think of. Nonnettes are little cakes made with honey and almonds — a delicious mixture that is all too easy to eat.

Fruit, especially soft fruit, plays an important part in the sweets of the region, and of course crème de cassis, the famous black currant liqueur is produced here. The combination of white wine and black currant liqueur called vin blanc cassis has long been a traditional Burgundian aperitif, but it was popularised by Dijon's deputy mayor, Canon Kir, in the 1940s to the point where his name has been adopted for the drink. The original proportions of one third cassis to two thirds Bourgogne Aligoté have been changed somewhat to reduce the amount of cassis. Other fruit liqueurs are still produced here, such as mirabelle and prunelle from plums, or fraise from strawberries but they tend to be overshadowed by cassis. Marc de Bourgogne is the local digestif, a spirit distilled from the skin and pips left after the final pressings of the wine. It can be quite heady and fiery, with a rather unsubtle flavour, but it has many devotees.

The wines themselves are a different matter for they include some of the greatest white and red wines in the world. There are five wine regions in Burgundy — from north to south Chablis, the Côte d'Or comprising the Côte de Nuits and the Côte de Beaune, the Côte Chalonnais, the Mâconnais and the Beaujolais. Four grapes are permitted, two red, the Pinot Noir and the Gamay; two white, the Chardonnay and the Aligoté. The Pinot Noir and the Chardonnay make the finest wines. The Pinot Noir does best in the Côte d'Or, producing elegant wines of great variety. The Chardonnay adapts quite well to the soils and climate of the

27

whole region and produces wines of distinctive character and finesse. The Gamay is the grape of Beaujolais and is little grown further north; the Aligoté, like the Chardonnay, grows throughout the region yielding crisp, dry wines. From these four grapes the whole range of red, white, rosé and sparkling wines is produced. Chablis, a hundred kilometres to the north of the main wine growing region, produces steely white wines that often have a flowery or new mown grass bouquet. The Grand Cru vineyards produce excellent wines, as do most of the Premiers Crus, but ordinary Chablis can be acidic and disappointing.

The Côte d'Or is the heart of Burgundy, with the wine trade centred on Beaune and Nuits-St-Georges. The vineyards are still very much a family business of small holdings. Some growers sell their grapes to négociant houses and leave them to make the wine, others make their own wine, perhaps selling a proportion in bulk to a négociant to finance the wine they mature and bottle themselves. This means that wines bearing the same name can vary greatly, according to the skill of the winemaker.

The Côte de Nuits begins just south of Dijon at Fixin and extends southwards for about twelve miles. Here are produced some of the greatest red wines in the world, such as Chambertin, Clos de Tart, Bonnes Mares, Clos de Vougeot, Romanée-Conti, La Tâche, Vosne-Romanée, wines of finesse and charm, with rich, generous depths and bouquet that may be reminiscent of violets or soft fruit, or in some cases of the farmyard, according to its origins and age.

More great red wines are made in the Côte de Beaune, but here are also the villages producing those extraordinary opulent white burgundies — Meursault, Puligny-Montrachet and Chassagne-Montrachet. Beaune itself is well worth a visit to see the Hôtel-Dieu and the wine museum. The third Sunday in November is the famous wine sale at the Hospices de Beaune, preceded by a banquet at Clos de Vougeot for the Chevaliers de Tastevin, one of the most important wine fraternities. The sale is followed by yet another banquet and a lunch known as La Paulée in Meursault on Monday. The events of the weekend are collectively called Les Trois Glorieuses.

Before moving south it is worth mentioning the wines now produced in the Hautes-Côtes to the west of the Côte because quality is improving and the wines are relatively inexpensive.

The Côte Chalonnaise is mostly planted with the Pinot Noir and villages such as

Rully, Mercury, Givry and Montagny produce fine, fruity, delicate wines. Bouzeron has its own appellation for Aligoté and the wine made here is fuller and richer than elsewhere. This region also produces some of the best sparkling Crémant de Bourgogne.

The Mâconnais has some chalky soil which suits the Chardonnay, the principal grape here, and a clay and sand region where the Gamay flourishes to make Mâcon Rouge. The red wine is usually drunk young, but the best white wines of Pouilly-Fuissé, Pouilly-Vinzelles, Pouilly-Loché and St-Véran are stylish and fruity and should keep for five years or more.

The Beaujolais is the most southerly vineyard and the largest. The best, the Beaujolais-Villages and the Crus, come from the northern part: the south tends to produce Beaujolais nouveau.

Many Burgundy vineyards are open to the public for tasting and sales, but think carefully before buying, for some growers charge tourists much more at the gate than you would pay in a shop.

Burgundy's wines are the obvious accompaniment to the food of the province; Beaujolais or Mâcon Rouge goes well with charcuterie; Meursault with jambon persillé, Chablis with goat's cheese, Aligoté with snails. A young red from the Côte de Beaune or the Côte Chalonnaise will partner a creamy poultry dish or oeufs en meurette; an older vintage will suit a coq au vin or boeuf à la bourguignonne and a great red burgundy will be superb with game.

Handy Tips

HOW TO GET THERE FROM THE UK
The Itinerary begins at Châtillon-sur-Seine, northern Burgundy. From the car ferry at Le Havre take the N182/A13 to Paris, and go south on the A6 to Auxerre and then the N965 to Châtillon. From the more southerly channel ports pick up the A26/A1 to Paris. Alternatively you might consider rail or air to Paris and then hiring a car. However, all channel crossings tend to become heavily booked, therefore we heartily recommend making an early reservation.

WHEN TO GO
Any time from Easter to the end of September. In a good Autumn, warm sunny weather will last to the end of October.

Try to avoid travelling on or just before or after a bank holiday (see below). The worst time for traffic is the first weekend in August, when nearly every French family is on the move.

HOTELS
It is advisable to book hotels in advance especially between July and September, particularly when your visit coincides with the wine festival.

CAMPING AND CARAVANNING
France is well provided with camp sites. Buy the green Michelin Camping and Caravanning guide for addresses. Unlike dreary England even the smallest of sites has electricity. N.B. Don't forget your Caravan Club of Great Britain registration carnet.

DRIVING
Driving on the right is usually no problem, the danger only comes when returning to the road from a car park, a petrol station and of course at roundabouts. Until recently priority was always given to those approaching from the right. This custom is fast changing and roundabouts can therefore be treated in the English style, but beware drivers turning from small roads in towns and country lanes. Traffic police can be tough even on foreign motorists

who are caught speeding, overshooting a red light or failing to wear seat belts, so take care. Seat belts are obligatory everywhere in France outside town limits.

ROAD NUMBERS

The French government, which used to be responsible for numbering all the roads in France, has started to hand over the responsibility to the individual départements. In their wisdom the individual départements have in some cases decided to renumber the roads and as you can imagine this process is not only slow but confusing. I have tried to be as correct as possible with the road numbers, but you may unfortunately find some discrepancies. For example you could come across a road marked as the N137 when it is really the D937.

SPEED LIMITS

Autoroutes	130 kmph (80 mph)
Other Roads	90 kmph (56 mph)
Dual Carriageways	110 kmph (68 mph)
Built-up areas or as directed by signs	60 kmph (37 mph)

Autoroutes nearly all have periodic tolls (péages) and can be expensive on long journeys.

THE METRIC SYSTEM

Kilometres— for road distances 8 km equals 5 miles thus:

Km:miles	Km:miles	Km:miles	Km:miles
3:2	8:5	40:25	90:56
4:2½	9:5½	50:31	100:62
5:3	10:6	60:37	125:78
6:3½	20:12	70:44	150:94
7:4	30:18	80:50	200:125

BANK HOLIDAYS

New Years' Day	1st January
Easter Monday	Variable
Labour Day	1st May
V.E. Day	8th May
Ascension Day	6th Thursday after Easter
Whit Monday	2nd Monday after Ascension
Bastille Day	14th July
Assumption	15th August
All Saints (Toussaint)	1st November

| Armistice Day | 11th November |
| Christmas Day | 25th December |

BANKS

Banks are shut on Saturdays and Sundays, except in towns with a Saturday market, when they open on Saturday and shut on Monday. Banks also close at midday on the eve of bank holidays. Banking hours are normally 8 a.m.-12 noon and 2-4.30 p.m. When changing cheques or travellers' cheques remember your passport and Eurocheque encashment card or other internationally recognised cheque card.

SHOP OPENING TIMES

These vary according to a) season b) type of shop c) size of town. In most places shops are open on Saturday, but may be shut on Monday. Food shops (baker, butcher, general store) tend to shut later than others, sometimes as late as 7 p.m., some open on Sundays and bank holiday mornings. Generally all shops close for 2-3 hours at lunchtime from midday.

TRANSPORT

S.N.C.F. — Société Nationale de Chemin de Fer. The trains are generally very clean, comfortable and punctual. It is best to buy tickets in advance from mainline stations or travel agents. Seats can be reserved on main lines. Hire cars can be booked in advance in most large towns. Bicycles can be hired at some stations. Men over 65 and women over 60 should purchase a Rail Europ S (RES), from British Rail. This will entitle you to a 50% reduction on fares. Hoverspeed (UK) and Sealink (UK) also provide reduced fares. Hoverspeed (UK) Ltd and Sealink (UK) Ltd also grant price reductions.

Note: Many stations have automatic red punch ticket machines on the platform, this dates your ticket. If you do not get your ticket punched by one of these machines you can be charged again, plus a fine of 20%, so be careful.

MONUMENTS AND MUSEUMS

Opening times and prices of admission have not been included in this book, as they are subject to change. All places mentioned are open to the public and will charge a few francs admission. Normally they will be open from Easter to the end of October, from 9.30-12.00 a.m. and from 3-5 p.m.

Note: Guided tours will cease admission half an hour before closing. Check with the local tourist office for details.

KEY TO ITINERARY
Ratings are for prices/room/night.

★★   Reasonable   ★★★★   Expensive

★★★   Average   ★★★★★   Very expensive

Names of the hotels and restaurants are printed in bold and are distinguished by the following symbols:

Lunch   Dinner

The Itinerary provides a basic route for each day and, for those with time available, offers suggestions for additional trips marked in the text as *Detours*.

Maps
The map on pp. 10-11 shows the complete Itinerary.
The daily routes are mapped in detail as follows:
Days 1-4:   p. 36
Days 5-9:   p. 71
Days 10-14:   pp. 106-7

At the beginning of each day in the Itinerary there is a summary of the day's route and grid references of the places to be visited. Grid references are given longitude first, then latitude (i.e. reading from the perimeter of the map, the horizontal numbers then the vertical). Each square represents 10′.

We recommend you use Michelin Series 1/200,000-1cm:2km, Map nos. 237, 238 and 243 (also 244 if you pursue the detour to Villefranche, pp. 83-4).

Châtillon-sur-Seine

The Itinerary

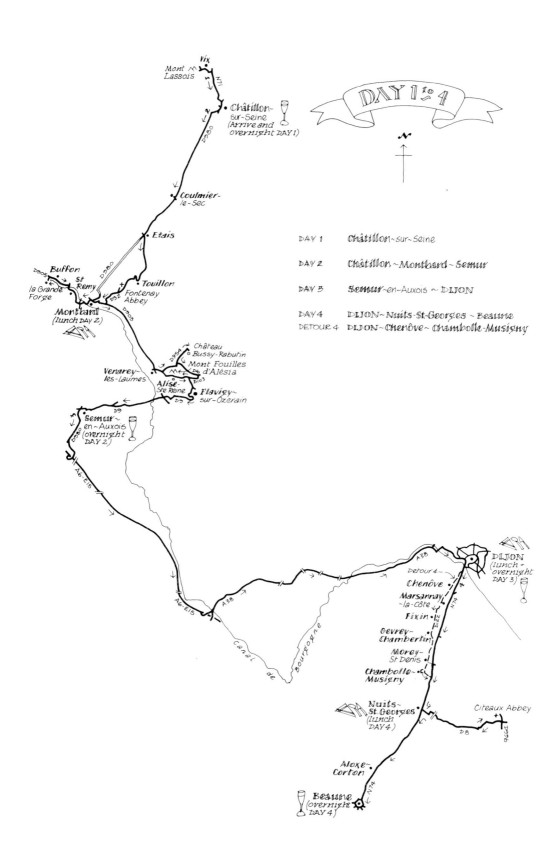

DAY 1 to 4

Vix
Mont Lassois
Châtillon-sur-Seine (Arrive and overnight DAY 1)
D980
Coulmier-le-Sec
Etais
D980
Buffon
la Grande Forge
St Remy
Touillon
Fontenay Abbey
D905
Montbard (lunch DAY 2)
D954
Château Bussy-Rabutin
Mont Fouilles d'Alésia
D103
Venarey-les-Laumes
Alise-Ste Reine
Flavigny-sur-Ozerain
D9
Semur-en-Auxois (overnight DAY 2)
D980
A6-E15
A6-E15
A38
A38
Canal de Bourgogne
Detour 4
Chenôve
Marsannay-la-Côte
Fixin
Gevrey-Chambertin
Morey-St Denis
Chambolle-Musigny
DIJON (lunch + overnight DAY 3)
N74
Nuits-St-Georges (lunch DAY 4)
Citeaux Abbey
D8
9604
Aloxe-Corton
N74
Beaune (overnight DAY 4)

DAY 1	Châtillon-sur-Seine
DAY 2	Châtillon ~ Montbard ~ Semur
DAY 3	Semur-en-Auxois ~ DIJON
DAY 4	DIJON~Nuits-St-Georges ~ Beaune
DETOUR 4	DIJON~Chenôve~ Chambolle-Musigny

DAY 1

The itinerary starts at Châtillon-sur-Seine in northern Burgundy. Châtillon is an agreeable riverside town where you can spend a relaxing afternoon soaking up the local atmosphere before commencing your tour.

Overnight at Châtillon-sur-Seine

Map references
Châtillon-sur-Seine   4°35′E 47°53′N
Vix   4°35′E 47°54′N

Arrive Châtillon-sur-Seine.

Châtillon-sur-Seine, a small pleasant town, standing at the confluence of the Seine and the Douix, and dominated by its sturdy, severely-grand 11th- to 13th-century church, St Vorles, is as good a place as any to start on your tour of Burgundy. Its centre, destroyed during the last war, has been rebuilt. The town was awarded the Croix de Guerre because of the heroism of its citizens.

Châtillon is chiefly renowned for its possession of the Trésor de Vix, a sensational post-war archaeological disovery, now housed in attractive 16th-century Renaissance, Maison Philandrier, which also contains one of the best collections of Gallo-Roman antiquities in Burgundy. About 7 kms north of Châtillon stands Mont Lassois and the village of Vix. The treasure, excavated from the site of a hill fort at Vix in 1953, was a bronze urn, as tall as a man, made by Grecian craftsmen, dating from about 500 BC. The burial chamber also held silver cups, and a funeral chariot enclosing the skeleton of a Gallic princess, adorned with bracelets, necklaces and a golden diadem.

Gallic princes were strongly established at Mont Lassois. It is believed that there was probably some sort of emporium here where trading routes met and at which merchandise was exchanged with traders who came from as far as Italy and Greece. More recently in 1914 General Joffre chose Châtillon as his headquarters.

Dinner and overnight at Châtillon-sur-Seine.

CHÂTILLON-SUR-SEINE: USEFUL INFORMATION

Tourist Office:	Place Marmont
	Tel: (80) 91 13 19
Population:	7,963
General interest:	Museum

Hôtel de la Côte d'Or
Rue Charles Ronot
21400 Châtillon-sur-Seine
Tel: (80) 91 13 39

A small, moderately priced hotel in a quiet but very central position, where you are assured of excellent care and attention from the patron who is also the chef.

Closed:	Fête Days, Sunday evenings and Mondays — except in July and August
Rooms:	11
Facilities:	Television in the rooms, restaurant
Credit cards:	Carte Bleu, Am.Ex, Diners, Visa, Euro, Mastercard
Food:	Good value
Rating:	★★★

Sylvia Hôtel
9 Avenue de la Gare
21400 Châtillon-sur-Seine
Tel: (80) 91 02 44

This hotel has the air of a grand country house set in its own grounds, and is approached through imposing entrance gates off the main road. Moderately priced but unfortunately no restaurant.

Closed:	Open all year
Rooms:	21
Credit cards:	Visa, Carte Bleu, Mastercard

DAY 2

Châtillon-sur-Seine, Fontenay Abbey, Montbard, Flavigny, Semur-en-Auxois: approx. 94 km (59 miles).

South of Châtillon the morning is spent at the beautifully sited and much restored Fontenay Abbey. After lunch by the canal at Montbard visit the ancient battleground of Alise-Ste-Reine, and the amusing but attractive château of Bussy-Rabutin. Heading west via the restored medieval town of Flavigny, the day ends at the fortress town of Semur-en-Auxois.

Overnight at Semur-en-Auxois.

Map references

Châtillon-sur-Seine	4°35′E 47°53′N
Fontenay Abbey	4°24′E 47°38′N
Montbard	4°21′E 47°37′N
Buffon	4°17′E 47°38′N
Venarey-les-Laumes	4°28′E 47°33′N
Alise-Ste-Reine	4°30′E 47°33′N
Bussy-Rabutin	4°32′E 47°34′N
Flavigny-sur-Ozerain	4°32′E 47°31′N
Semur-en-Auxois	4°20′E 47°29′N

Route shown p. 36.

Semur-en-Auxois

Breakfast at Châtillon.

Depart Châtillon-sur-Seine (D980) via Coulmier and Etais (20 kms). Turn here toward Touillon and on to Fontenay Abbey (D32).

Fontenay Abbey

At the far end of a valley, surrounded by softly wooded hills, stands the old abbey of Fontenay, a perfect example of a Cistercian abbey. Simple, austere, with no ornamentation to distract, it blends most harmoniously into its leafy background.

Fontenay was founded by St Bernard in 1118 after he had been Abbot of Clairvaux and, from the 12th to the 15th century, it was one of the most prosperous and powerful abbeys in France. Decadence set in when abbots were appointed by royal favour. Disorders brought about by the religious wars hastened its decline. During the French Revolution, the abbey was converted into a paper mill. Paper was produced here until 1906, when restoration took place and the new owners had the abbey returned to its 12th-century glory. The same family, the Aynards, are still responsible for its maintenance, although it is now designated as a historical monument. It was classified as 'Universal Heritage' by UNESCO in 1981.

One enters the monastery by a two-storey gatehouse, once the lodgings of the monk porter. To see inside is the wayfarers' chapel, and bakery; the abbot's lodging house; the kennel, where the Dukes of Burgundy kept their dogs while hunting in the surrounding forest; the church (built quickly between 1139 and 1147, and the oldest Cistercian one in France), the dormitory, a communal one, where monks slept without heat on straw mattresses on the floor; the cloister, the heart of the abbey; the Council room where the monks assembled for meetings; the copying room where they copied manuscripts during the winter; the detention room, the abbey's prison; the infirmary near the herb garden; the forge, a sort of factory where tools were made. The refectory, probably once a magnificent building, alas destroyed, has not been reconstructed. The hostel, once used for pilgrims, is now a farm.

Incidentally, Fontenay takes its name from the fountains you will see in its parks. Here you will find a famous trout hatchery. Trouts were traditionally served by the monks to the Dukes of Burgundy.

Visits to the abbey take the form of guided tours, lasting about 40 minutes. It is open every day.

Fontenay is the centre of an interesting region with plenty of châteaux and historical towns to visit.

Take the D32/905 to Montbard.

Montbard, built on a hill, once the site of a castle belonging to the Counts, then the Dukes, of Burgundy, is now an important metallurgical centre and a port on the canal de Bourgogne.

George Louis le Clerc, Comte de Buffon (1707-88) has often been blamed for the destruction of the castle. But in fact it was already mostly in ruins when he acquired it in the 18th century. The town owes more to him and his memory than it does to the men of war.

Even as a boy Buffon was passionately interested in science, visiting Italy, Switzerland and England in order to pursue his studies. When he was appointed Keeper of the Royal Gardens in Paris and was obliged to spend four months of the year in the capital, he was always glad to get back to his study in the castle grounds, where he devoted his energies to writing his *Histoire Naturelle*.

Although Buffon had most of the remaining castle destroyed, he built himself a comfortable house, Hôtel de Buffon, which was connected to his study by a bridge. The 52-metre Tour de l'Aubespin, from which there is a beautiful view, still stands, also Tour St Louis, which holds souvenirs of the great naturalist, as does the small pavilion which was his study. He is buried in the little chapel, adjoining the church, St Urse, beyond the park, which is now a public promenade. Buffon was a pioneer of industry as well of natural history, and in 1768 he set up a model ironworks at the nearby village from which he derived his title. This may well be the reason why Montbard became an industrial town. The Grande Forge at Buffon (6 kms north along D905) has been lovingly restored and is an impressive sight by the canal. It is open during the summer.

Lunch at Montbard/St Remy.

Take the D905 to Venarey-les-Laumes, and the D103 to Alise-Ste-Reine.

Alise-Ste-Reine

The whole of this area is called Alésia and includes the site where the last important battle took place between the Gauls and Romans. If you walk up the hill to the summit of Mont Auxois, you will pass the Théâtre des Roches, where the Mystère de Ste Reine is performed annually during the September pilgrimage. Ste Reine was a shepherdess saint, martyred during the third century because she refused to marry a Roman centurion.

Mont Auxois, topped by a large bronze statue of Vercingétorix (by Millet), might be called the tomb of Celtic France and the cradle of the French nation. Nearby a landmark indicator shows a map of the site. Caesar had 40,000 men when the memorable siege began. It lasted six weeks and he surrounded Vercingétorix' strongly-defended fort with trenches, walls, pallisades or stakes and towers, so that none could leave or enter. When Vercingétorix finally surrendered, there were so many men in his force that each legionary had a string of captives. When Vercingétorix himself emerged, he was wearing the golden armour of a Gallic chieftain, carrying his finest weapons, while his horse was caparisoned as if for a fête. After he had ridden round Caesar, he halted, dismounted, disarmed himself and knelt in front of him. His fate was to be taken to Rome in chains and paraded through the streets. He was murdered six years later.

Excavations carried out here in the last century have revealed traces of military works, bones of horses and men, coins and weapons, remains of Gallic living quarters, Roman baths, theatre, temple and forum and a basilica dedicated to Ste Reine.

You can visit the excavations, which are still going on, of the Gallic Roman town centre west of Auxois and a small museum. They are both open from spring to the 1st November.

If you take the D954 eastwards, you will come to the château of Bussy-Rabutin, standing on a wooded hillside.

Bussy-Rabutin

Repeated indiscretions and vanity dogged the life of Roger de Bussy-Rabutin (1618-1693). His pen especially was always landing him in trouble. He was banished to his estate in Burgundy after singing couplets ridiculing the young

Louis XIV's sad love affair with Marie Mancini. After writing a love history of the Gauls, a satire on the love affairs of the court, he was even sent to the Bastille, before being banished to his estate again.

When at home he spent much of his time on interior decorations. These efforts could not be described as great but they are entertaining. In the Salle des Devises (room of epigrams) where panels illustrate allegorical subjects, he himself appears as the reed that bends but does not break. In the Salon des Grands Hommes de Guerre are the portraits of 65 warriors ranging from Du Guesclin (famous Breton general) to De Bussy himself. His bedroom is hung with portraits of famous royal mistresses and members of his own family. But the circular Tour Dorée is the piece de résistance. Its walls are covered from walls to ceilings with paintings. There are important personages from the courts of Louis XIII and Louis XIV, the kings and cardinals, princes, mythological subjects and portraits of the most beautiful women in society, spicely captioned.

Flavigny-sur-Ozerain

Retrace your journey along D954, turn onto the D6/10, and Flavigny-sur-Ozerain should loom up on the other side of the valley, standing on a rocky promontory above the river and two tributaries.

During medieval times, Flavigny was one of Burgundy's most important fortified cities and became a sort of provincial government. But when the nobles and bourgeois left, it deteriorated. Recently it has come back to life. Many old houses have been restored. Antique and curio shops have been installed in some of the decrepit old buildings. Apart from exploring Flavigny's narrow streets, find time to visit St Génest church and the remains of the 8th-century abbey of St Pierre.

Leave from the Porte du Bourg and make for Semur, capital of the Auxois, and another old fortress town.

Semur-en-Auxois

Here old houses rise in terraces topped by four towers and the spire of Notre-Dame, above ramparts and the meandering Armançon. It has been compared to the Athenian acropolis. Legend says it was founded by Hercules.

Four towers are all that remain of its once impregnable fortress which was destroyed by Louis XI after a long siege. On the death of Duke Charles the Rash, the town unwisely supported his daughter Mary against the French king. You can visit the Tour de l'Orle and d'Or and the museum (geology, archaeology and folklore) and stroll along the ramparts which have been converted into shaded promenades. The Gothic church of Notre-Dame (founded 11th century) — a miniature cathedral — contains a fine polychrome, sculpted about 1490, showing the burial of Christ. The municipal library, lodged in the grounds of the Dominican convent, has a rare selection of early manuscripts and a gold-lettered missal which belonged to Anne of Brittany on display.

A good view of the medieval city may be had from Pont Joly, especially in the evening.

Overnight at Semur.

Le St Remy
St Remy
21500 Montbard
Tel: (80) 92 13 44

4 km northwest of Montbard, this is a spacious and airy restaurant, with spectacular beamed ceiling and archway. Well worth the extra journey. It would be difficult to overspend at lunchtime with three fixed price menus all offering a marvellous choice.

Closed:	19 December-23 January, evenings, except Saturday, and Mondays
Credit cards:	Carte Bleu, Am.Ex, Diners
Food:	Specialities include Le Saupiquet Montbardois de M. Bellin and Les Oeufs en Meurette.
Rating:	★★

If you wish to remain in the centre of Montbard there is:

Hôtel-Restaurant de l'Ecu
7 Rue Auguste Carré
21500 Montbard
Tel: (80) 92 11 66

A handsome medium-sized hotel in the centre of town close to the river. The cosy dining room offers a wide range of menus from very reasonable to quite expensive.

Closed:	Open all year
Credit cards:	Am.Ex, Diners, Visa, Euro
Food:	Interesting, e.g. Pigeon roasted with garlic or Fillet steak with olive oil followed by pancakes stuffed with nougat.
Rating:	★★★

MONTBARD: USEFUL INFORMATION

Tourist Office:	Rue Carnot
	Tel: (80) 92 03 75
Population:	7,916
General Interest:	Parc Buffon

Hôtel Les Cymaises
7 Rue de Renaudot
21140 Semur-en-Auxois
Tel: (80) 97 21 44

A solid, ancient-looking establishment with all modern facilities and a delightful walled garden. Although it has no restaurant of its own, the patron recommends eating at 'La Cambuse' or 'Le Carillon' nearby.

Hotel des Cymaises *contd.*

Closed:	15 February to 1 March
Rooms:	11
Facilities:	Garden, parking
Credit cards:	Euro, Visa
Rating:	★★

Hôtel du Lac
Lac de Pont
21140 Semur-en-Auxois
Tel: (80) 97 11 11

Closed:	Sunday evenings and Mondays except in July and August
Rooms:	29
Credit cards:	Carte Bleu, Diners
Food:	Typically Burgundian
Rating:	★★

SEMUR-EN-AUXOIS: USEFUL INFORMATION

Tourist Office:	Place Gaveau
	Tel: (80) 97 05 96
Population:	5,364
General Interest:	Lovely views

DAY 3

Semur-en-Auxois, Dijon: approx. 80 km (50 miles)

The day is spent in Dijon — where there is much to see, particularly the architecture in the old quarter, visit, and taste. Dijon is justifiably renowned for its gastronomic delights, here you are assured of good meals served with excellent wines.

Map references
Semur-en-Auxois   4°20′E 47°29′N
Dijon   5°03′E 47°18′N

Route shown p. 36.

Dijon

Travels in Burgundy

Breakfast at Semur-en-Auxois.

Take the D980 and the A6-E15/A38 to Dijon.

Dijon, capital of the crossroads of great highways, chief city of the great dukes, has always been a traveller's town. Even in the 17th century, it had over 200 hotels. Today, an important stopping-place for tourists on their way south, it is a pleasantly mellowed, quite busy town with some excellent museums, churches and fine Renaissance houses to see. It is also a centre of good eating: two Dijon specialities are gingerbread and mustard (a major export). A famous gastronomic fair takes place here every November.

At Dijon you will know you're in the south. The town has a lethargic somewhat sluggish atmosphere. Everyone, everywhere, seems to take their time — in the banks, shops, restaurants and cafés. There is a feeling of 'laissez-faire'. You will soon get used to it — you will have to! After all, you're on holiday.

Start your tour of the town from the main Tourist Office in Place Darcy. There is an official tour in English but only at certain times on certain days. In any case it is more pleasant to explore on one's own. Note: you can buy one ticket in Dijon which allows you to visit most of the museums.

You will first note the shaded leafy park with its statue of a polar bear by Pompon, Burgundy's renowned animal sculptor. Further on, the 18th-century Arc de Triomphe, Porte Guillaume, erected in honour of a Prince of Condé, a governor of the province, marks the entrance to Rue de la Liberté, which runs through the heart of the old city.

Turn left down Rue D. Maret, which leads to Place St Benigné, and its cathedral and one time Bénédictine abbey, destroyed and rebuilt four times. This last version was constructed between 1280 and 1314. Its most striking features are two massive towers, their conical roofs covered by different coloured tiles, and the 9th- to 11th-century crypt, a masterpiece of Romanesque art. Down here you will find the sarcophagus of the first local martyr, Saint Benigné, around which the rotunda, the original church, was built. There is an archaeological museum next door to the church.

Situated nearby in Rue Michelet (named after a famous French historian) is Romanesque 12th-century St Philibert, restored in the 15th, surmounted by a Gothic spire. Continue towards Rue Bossuet, passing the theatre and some interesting old houses, and back to Rue de la Liberté.

The small cobbled square, surrounded by old houses on the other side of road, was dedicated to the memory of François Rude, and is popularly known as Place de Bareuzai (dialect for wine-grower) after the statue of the naked man treading grapes. All around here is delightful for strolling, for you are now in the really old part of town. Rue des Forges in particular is one of the most characteristic. Along Rue de la Chouette, No. 8, is the Hôtel de Vogué, early 17th-century with its Renaissance portico this is often called the most beautiful of the Parliamentary town houses. Note the 15th-century half-timbered houses along Rue Verrerie. Most of Dijon's main points of interest to visitors are to be seen in this area.

Place de Libération, formerly called Place Royale, opens out into a graceful semicircle (now filled with cars) in front of the Palais des Ducs, later known as the Palais des Etats. The large statue of Louis XIV which once stood here was destroyed during the Revolution. The Place and the Palais were transformed in the 17th and 18th centuries. The Dijonnais, feeling that the town should be a proper capital again, had the ducal palace — abandoned since the death of Charles the Rash — restored, but in the classical style. The rebuilding was carried out by pupils of Mansart. The best place to view the Palais is from the Place Ducs de Bourgogne.

The Fine Arts museum which shares this imposing group of buildings with the Town Hall, is one of the oldest and richest in France. The collection is very well-organised. On the ground floor is sculpture and Burgundian art, on the upper floors, collections of paintings arranged in different schools. The best, in my view, is the modern art section. But while the rest of the museum is open all day (doesn't close for lunch) you may have to wait for this to open.

Don't miss the kitchen and the Guard Room. Two Dukes of Burgundy, John the Fearless and Philip the Bold, have their tombs in the Salle des Gardes, built by Philip the Bold at the height of his power. The marble figures of John the Fearless and his wife, Marguerite of Bavaria, lie side by side, presided over by angels with golden wings, a lion at their feet. Philip the Bold lies in similar magnificent state. They were worked on by Jean de Marville, Claus Sluter and Claus de Werve. John the Fearless's body, hastily buried at Montereau, was reclaimed by a Burgundian raiding party.

These monuments were originally situated in the Chartreuse de Champol (Carthusian monastery), which was founded by Philip the Bold, and intended as a ducal necropolis. When François I was taken to Champol, he requested that the coffin of John the Fearless be opened, so that he might see his remains. 'Through that hole,' a monk said, pointing to the shattered skull, 'the English entered France.'

Behind the Palais des Ducs are the gardens and narrow streets of the old town whose names recall some of the trade guilds; also Notre-Dame, Dijon's 13th-century church with its graceful bell tower, which houses the giant bell brought back from Courtrai in Flanders by Philip the Bold after he had quelled his subjects there in 1382. The Dijonnais became rather fond of the little man in the cocked hat who struck the bell with his hammer every hour. In 1500, they gave him a name 'Jacquemart'. Eventually, it was decided that he needed a wife to help him strike and in 1610, a woman was added. In 1714, the couple were presented with a son, Jacquelinet, to strike the half hour, and in 1881, a daughter, Jacquelinette, to strike the quarters. Unfortunately this treasure is old and often needs repair so it is frequently surrounded by scaffolding.

Another interesting feature of Notre-Dame is the 11th-century Black Virgin, known as 'Our Lady of Good Hope', the town's protectress, who is supposed to have twice come to Dijon's rescue. The first time was in 1513 when an army of 30,000 Swiss and German soldiers (sent by Marguerite of Austria, daughter of Mary of Burgundy, in an attempt to recover her grandfather's duchy from the French king) were besieging the city. After the despairing townspeople had prayed to the Black Virgin, their governor had an idea. Negotiators sent to parley with the besiegers, hospitably offered them wine, and before long the enemy were too fuddled to know what they were doing. They eventually agreed to go away if the Dijonnais paid them a large sum of money and if the French king would evacuate Milan (needless to say he didn't).

The other occasion was during the Second World War. German troops prepared to make a stand against the Americans in front of Dijon. The townspeople, afraid that their town would be destroyed during the fighting, again prayed to their Black Virgin. Suddenly and unexpectedly, the Germans withdrew. The Black Virgin may be seen, crowned, dressed in robes, in a side chapel.

Tapestries were made to commemorate these two occasions. The first one is in the Musée des Beaux Arts. The second one, which shows both these events, is hung inside Notre-Dame.

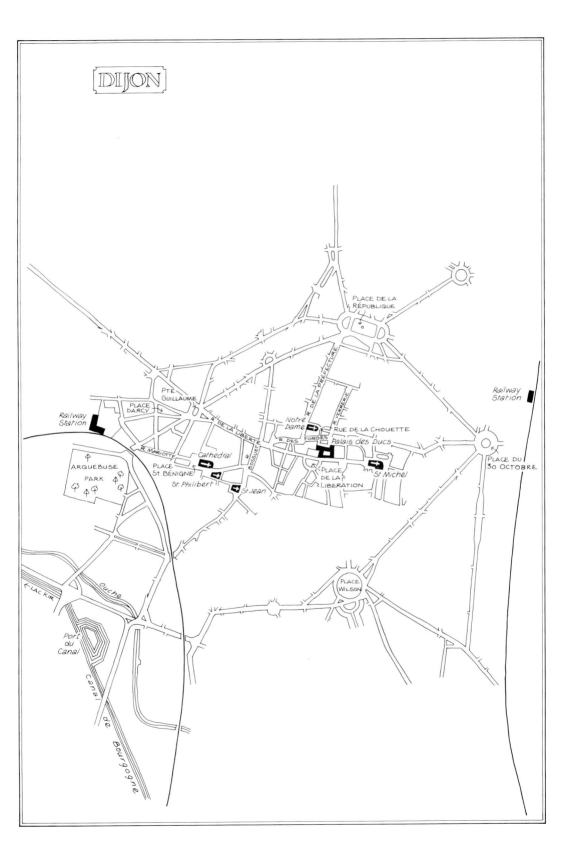

The other churches to see are St Michel (1499-1540) reputed to have the most harmonious Renaissance facade of all the churches in France, and St Jean (pure flamboyant style).

You might also care to visit the Arquebuse park, not far from the station. Apart from its gardens of rare plants it has a museum of natural history. If you wish to visit the Chartreuse de Champol to see statuary by Sluter, you will have to drive there from the station along Albert Avenue, about 5 kms. It was destroyed in 1793 during the French Revolution and has been replaced by a psychiatric hospital. The gates are usually open, viewing is free, and you drive through following the signs, leaving your car in the car park. To see is the Puits des Moise (Moses Well) and a very ornamental 15th-century chapel door.

For a change of pace, Lake Kir on the western edge of town offers a variety of water sports and you can walk back towards the centre along the Coulée Vert, a specially constructed pathway along the banks of the River Ouche, to Port du Canal. Here in summer the small moorings are packed with river barges and pleasure boats.

Detour

The next couple of days of the Itinerary will be spent travelling through one of the most prestigious wine regions in the world. As this obviously means that your chosen driver will miss many of the wines, you might consider a one-day bus tour of the region before continuing the Itinerary. The Dijon Tourist Office organises tasting tours about twice a week. One I would recommend is the one of the vineyards, organised by Bourgogne Tours in rue de la Liberté, every Thursday. It is fairly pricey but the cost includes the coach journey to Beaune and back, a good four-course lunch with wine, two wine tastings, one at Clos de Vougeot and one at Beaune (37 wines; the best ones are last), visit to Hôtel Dieu, and a short tour of Dijon at the end. And there is an English commentary. It would give the driver a chance to sample the wines without having to worry about his condition at the end.

Lunch and overnight at Dijon.

For lunch this stunningly situated restaurant is a must.

Restaurant Le Vinarium
23 Place Bossuet
21000 Dijon
Tel: (80) 30 36 23

Set in a spectaclar stone-vaulted crypt said to date from the 13th century. The enterprising menu includes four menus from the regions of Burgundy — Dijon, Mâcon, Niverne, Auxerre or a seasonal menu from the local covered market, not to mention à la carte. There is a short aperitif list based on Burgundy wines with fruit liqueurs.

Closed:	Sundays and Monday lunchtimes
Credit cards:	Carte Bleu, Am.Ex, Diners, Visa
Food:	Interesting with strong regional emphasis. Try crepes stuffed with Burgundian snails.
Rating:	★★

Spend the night at:

Hostellerie du Chapeau Rouge
5 Rue Michelet
21000 Dijon
Tel: (80) 30 28 10

A smart and luxurious hotel with elegant dining room, especially noted for its cellar of good wines of the area.

Closed:	Open all year
Rooms:	30
Facilities:	Restaurant
Credit cards:	Am.Ex, Diners, Visa, Euro
Food:	A typical menu offers Duckling breast with cream and mushroom sauce, Pork with lemon sauce or salmon 'pinot noir et à la Moelle'.
Rating:	★★★★

Hôtel Montigny
8 Rue Montigny
21000 Dijon
Tel: (80) 30 96 86

A pleasant if small hotel close to the town centre.

Closed:	Open all year
Rooms:	30
Facilities:	Bar, parking, rooms with handicapped access, dogs
Credit cards:	Euro
Rating:	★★

Hôtel Les Rosiers
22bis Rue de Montchapet
21000 Dijon
Tel: (80) 55 33 11

Closed:	Open all year
Rooms:	10
Credit cards:	Carte Bleu, Am.Ex
Rating:	★★

DIJON: USEFUL INFORMATION

Tourist Office:	Place Darcy
	Tel: (80) 43 42 12
Population:	145,569
Facilities:	Water sports (Lake Kir), Golf course (10 kms)
General Interest:	Museums, cathedral, old buildings and gardens

DAY 4

Dijon, Nuits-St-Georges, Beaune: approx. 40 km (25 miles)

Today is almost entirely devoted to wine. In the morning the route follows the Côte de Nuits. Vineyards surround you and many producers offer opportunities for tastings and short tours, just watch for the signs telling which are open for visitors on the day you pass. After visiting Clos de Vougeot, head to Nuits-St-Georges for lunch. Continuing south the rest of the afternoon can be spent at Beaune.

Overnight at Beaune.

Map references
Dijon   5°03′E 47°18′N
Close de Vougeot   4°56′E 47°11′N
Nuits-St-Georges   4°56′E 47°18′N
Beaune   4°51′E 47°02′N

Detour 1
Marsanny-la-Côte   4°59′E 47°16′N
Fixin   4°58′E 47°14′N
Morey-St-Denis   4°57′E 47°12′N

Detour 2
Cîteaux Abbey   5°06′E 47°18′N

Route shown p. 36

Travels in Burgundy

Breakfast at Dijon.

Leave Dijon on the N74 heading south.

Detour 1

Some of the major vineyards are by the N74, others are off to the right. If you have extra time you could take the D122 (parallel to N74) to Clos de Vougeot which puts you more directly in contact with such villages as Marsannay-la-Côte (rosé), Fixin (La Perrière, Clos de Chapitre, Les Hervelets) Morey-St-Denis, and Chambolle-Musigny.

Burgundy's wine regions

Vines were planted in Burgundy long before the Romans arrived, but the greatest number of vineyards were planted after the 12th century, when monks, particularly Cistercians, cleared the land they had been bequeathed of forests and reclaimed harsh untilled land. Long years of hard labour and patience laid the foundations for the vineyards. The Dukes of Burgundy, who proclaimed that they were the lords of the best wine in Christendom, served it at magnificent banquests and sent it as gifts to foreign countries, thereby spreading the fame of Burgundy wine through Europe.

Burgundy has about 126,000 acres of vineyards, about half of which produce good wines. They can be divided into five major regions; Chablis, the Côte d'Or (which comprises the Côte de Nuits and the Côte de Beaune), the Côte de Chalon, the Mâconnais and the Beaujolais.

This lies roughly between the towns of Dijon and Chagny, a stretch of about 54 kms, the Triumphal Way of the Great Wines. The vineyards grow in terraces on the sunny slopes of hills (côtes). In summer, the lines of green foliage contrast strongly with the reddish-brown earth. In autumn, when their leaves have turned golden brown, you will understand why this area has been aptly named the Côte d'Or.

Here are the greatest wine-growing vineyards in Burgundy, not so much for quantity as for their quality. The Côte d'Or divides into two main parts, the Côte de Nuits and the Côte de Beaune (plus the hautes Côtes, an area of high hills in the west). There are a few vineyards grouped under the name Côte Dijonnais, near Dijon. These are the remains of a vast vineyard that was devastated by phylloxera, a small beetle from America, which wrought havoc in Burgundy's, and indeed Europe's vineyards, during the last century. The vines were finally saved by French plants being grafted on to American vines, which were immune to the disease caused by the beetle.

The Côte de Nuits begins at Dijon, following the National Highway 74, named Routes des Grands Crus, and ends at Corgoloin. It produces the great red wines, rich and robust and which take 10 to 12 years to mature. A few well-known names are Chambertin, Clos de Vougeot, Vosne-Romanée and Nuits-St-Georges. The Côte de Beaune produces great white wines. Two famous ones are Mersault and Montrachet (some say the greatest white wine in the world). Its reds are smooth, but less full-blooded than those of the Côte de Nuits. They also mature more rapidly, but grow old earlier.

Incidentally, along the road you will see plenty of places where you can stop and taste the wine. Obviously the producers would prefer you purchased some of their stock but there is rarely any compulsion to do so. Some cellars charge a small fee — this usually includes a short guided tour and is often very worthwhile.

Côte de Nuits' main attraction is the château du Clos de Vougeot, now the property of the Confrérie des Chevaliers du Tastevin, a group of merchants and wine growers, who bought it in 1934 in order to publicise their wines. Banquets are held here. Every January there is a famous ceremony in honour of St Vincent, patron saint of Vignerons. The château, a plain building, built in 1551, which belonged to the monks until the Revolution, stands out amongst the vineyards. It is open to the public for tours, wine-tastings and meals. Beside the château stands the 13th-century cellar and vat rooms, where you can see four of the original 13th-century wine presses. Clos de Vougeot, the wine, was originally created by the monks of Cîteaux. The best of it was never sold but given as presents to crowned heads and important dignitaries. Its fame was such that during the Revolutionary Wars, a Colonel Bisson and his troops halted and gave the wine full military honours. This later became a military tradition.

Further along the N74 come the vineyards of Vosne-Romanée, which produces some of the world's most expensive wines. Next is the important town of Nuits-

St-Georges, a town where everyone seems connected with the wine trade; it is the end and the commercial centre of the Côtes de Nuits. A major annual event is the auction of wines donated to the Hospice St Laurent. The Hospice (17th-century) deals primarily with care of the aged. You might care to visit the 13th-century church of St Symporien.

Lunch at Nuits-St-Georges.

Detour

If time you could make a detour to Cîteaux, D8, D996, one of the principal sites of Christianity, now much reduced in size and importance. It was founded in 1098 by three monks in search of a desolate place away from the world in which they could devote their lives to prayer and hard labour. They settled here amongst the cistel reeds, hence the name 'Cîteaux'. At first, it failed to prosper but was brought to life by the indomitable St Bernard of Clairvaux and his followers who arrived here in 1114. A huge Cistercian expansion took place. About one hundred years later there were over 1000 Cistercian houses.

Alas, very little remains of the original monastery, which was sacked, exploited and finally supressed in 1790 when it was put to secular use. In 1898 it was restored to the status of Mother House of the Order and reformed Cistercians, now Trappists, returned. Their routine follows that laid down by St Bernard.

Visitors, but only men, are allowed every afternoon except Sundays and holidays. The monks make a very good cheese which is on sale here.

Return to N74 by D8.

Beaune

Beaune, seat of the Dukes of Burgundy, is the capital of Burgundy wine. It is still surrounded by its old ramparts, somewhat crumbling now though — towers and bastions of the 13th, 15th and 16th centuries. When visiting here, I did the Tour des Fosses (tour of ditches) shaded by plane trees, on foot, but alas arrived too late at Porte-St-Nicholas, an old gateway, to sample wine at La Reine Pédaque — one of the town's many wine cellars. You can get their addresses and times of opening and closing from the Tourist Office facing the Hôtel Dieu, and plan your tour of the town accordingly.

Apart from wine-tasting in Beaune a visit to the famous Hôtel Dieu is a must. Nicholas Rolin spent most of his life in the service of the Dukes of Burgundy. As chancellor, he combined a number of important functions, such as being Minister of Finance, so that he himself became very rich. In 1443, wishing to help Beaune, his mother's birthplace, to recover from the misery of the Hundred Years' War, he decided to build a hospital for the poor. Perhaps he was also thinking of his own salvation. As Louis XI ironically remarked 'having made so many people poor he had to make his peace with the Almighty by providing for some of them.'

The exterior of the Hospices de Beaune is sober. Its long plain grey stone facade is overshadowed by the steep grey slate roof. However, once through the entrance and in its main courtyard, the Cour d'Honneur, one is in a different, medieval world. A gallery runs below the picturesque array of dormer windows, chimney-pots and turrets. The varnished, many-coloured intricately patterned tiled roof sparkles in the bright light.

One's tour begins in the Grande Salle (72 metres long and its ceiling resembling an upturned ship). There is a chapel at the end as Rolin believed that the sick should be able to follow services. In the 15th century it held two rows of 31 beds, two patients per bed. Tables and benches for meals were in the centre. Pewter dishes were used.

Look for tiles on the floor which are decorated with the initials N and G (Nicholas and Guigone) and Seulle (alone). They represent the great affection that Nicholas felt for his wife, a very worthy woman of many good works who is buried in the chapel.

To see also is the linen room, the kitchen, the pharmacy (note collection of Nevers jugs and fine collection of pewter ware), the Salle St Louis, once a ward, and which now acts as a sort of vestibule to the new room, built to house the Polyptych of 'The Last Judgement'.

It was originally commissioned by Rolin to hang in the Great Hall, to help patients to bear their sufferings. It was removed during the Revolution, forgotten perhaps for years, then re-discovered, taken down and cleaned.

The Polyptych, when opened, reveals 9 different-sized panels. The centre one shows Christ. Four angels at his feet and either side of the Archangel Michael, announce the Last Judgement and awaken the dead. The apostles, John the Baptist and various other people, such as Philip the Good, the Pope, and yes, even Nicholas Rolin himself, his wife and possibly his daughter, fill the panels either side. At the bottom are the dead: those on the right make their way towards salvation; those on the left to the flames of Hell.

When the Hospices de Beaune was built, Rolin and his wife ensured its continued income by endowing it with vineyards which produce wine of very high quality. These are auctioned annually on the third Sunday in November with much pomp in the market hall — it used to be done in the courtyard of Hôtel Dieu — as the chief event of the Trois Glorieuses. Banquets are presided over by the Chevaliers of the noble fraternity of Tastevins. Auctions are still held à la chandelle. That is, a candle is lit at the start of the bidding and is put out when the bidding stops.

Also to see at Beaune is the interesting museum of Burgundy wine, situated in the old mansion of the Dukes of Burgundy (14th-, 15th- and 16th-century) and the nearby church of Notre-Dame, Burgundian Romanesque (frescoes and tapestries), nearby.

Beaune, popular with tourists, makes a good centre for excursions. To the west lies the Montagne de Beaune, Les Hautes Côtes de Beaune and village and château of Rochepot, the perfect knightly castle on its rocky height. Further west still is the hilly Morvan. To the east is the Jura. Southwards lie the vineyards of Chalonnaise, Mâconnais, Nivernais and Beaujolais.

Overnight at Beaune.

Le Caveau Saint Vincent
Avenue Charles de Gaulle
21700 Nuits-St-Georges
Tel: (80) 61 14 91

A modern looking establishment on the road south out of Nuits-St-Georges; however, inside the decor is based on an old Burgundian cellar with lovely stonevaulting. The plainness of the furnishings allows you to concentrate on the gastronomic and visual delights of the food. There is also a shop attached where you can buy wine and all sorts of regional produce.

Closed:	Monday evenings and Tuesdays
Credit cards:	Visa, Access, Euro
Rating:	★★★

NUITS-ST-GEORGES: USEFUL INFORMATION

Tourist Office:	Rue Sonays
	Tel: (80) 61 22 47
Population:	5,461
General Interest:	Wine tastings

Hôtel le Cep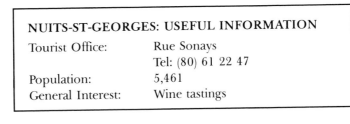
27 Rue Maufoux
21200 Beaune
Tel: (80) 22 35 48

Treat yourself to a luxurious night in this old hotel, once a private house, in the centre of Beaune. The bedrooms are lavish and beautifully furnished in classic French style. The hotel is an architectural treat with its own arcaded courtyard, ancient beamed reception rooms and cosy breakfast rooms in the old vaulted cellars. This is a top class hotel and you could pay a lot for a fantastic suite and the gastronomic menu for dinner, but you can still enjoy the stylish atmosphere if you accept the cheaper rooms and the reasonable fixed price menu.

Closed:	Open all year
Rooms:	49
Facilities:	Minibars and televisions in all rooms, restaurant
Credit cards:	Am.Ex, Diners, Visa, Euro, Mastercard, Access
Food:	Specialities — Pigeon de Bresse

Hôtel le Cep *contd.*

	Perigourdin, Gateau de Foies Blonds et son Coulis de Truffes
Rating:	★★★★

1 km from the centre of town:

Hôtel le Grillon
21 Route de Seurre
21200 Beaune
Tel: (80) 22 44 25

Closed:	Wednesday evenings (restaurant)
Rooms:	78
Facilities:	Restaurant
Credit cards:	Am.Ex, Diners, Visa
Food:	Simple, sensible food
Rating:	★★

BEAUNE: USEFUL INFORMATION

Tourist Office:	Opposite Hôtel Dieu, corner of Place de la Halle Tel: (80) 22 24 51
Population:	21,127
General Interest:	Wine, Museum, tastings, ramparts, Hospices

DAY 5

Beaune, Chagny, Chalon-sur-Saône, Tournus: approx. 64 km (40 miles)

The day's journey passes through some more prestigious wine areas and also some lesser known ones. Leave Beaune after another look round and lunch by the river at Chalon-sur-Saône, a leisurely, elegant old town. Then travel through the charming, hilly region of the Mâconnais to Tournus. If time take a circular tour to the dramatically situated Brancion.

Overnight at Tournus.

Map references

Beaune	4°51'E 47°02'N
Pommard	4°48'E 47°01'N
Volnay	4°47'E 47°00'N
Meursault	4°46'E 46°58'N
Chagny	4°45'E 46°55'N
Chalon-sur-Saône	4°52'E 46°47'N
Tournus	4°55'E 46°34'N

Detour

Brancion	4°48'E 46°33'N
Chapaize	4°46'E 46°34'N
Cormatin	4°41'E 46°33'N

Route shown p. 71.

Breakfast at Beaune.

You may wish to spend the morning exploring Beaune in which case I suggest you take the autoroute direct to Chalon for lunch. Alternatively the slower route between Beaune and Chalon provides ample opportunity to pay homage to more of the great names in wine.

Take the N74/D973 from Beaune to Pommard and continue up the hillside to Volnay. Turning left through Meursault, capital of the Côte de Blancs, continue on the N74 to Chagny — passing Puligny-Montrachet en route.

Chagny

Chagny, both an industrial town and a holiday resort, situated beside the Dheune and crossed by the Canal du Centre, lies on the boundary of the Saône et Loire region. A road and rail centre, it also marks the end of the Côte d'Or. Although the vineyards to its south are less important than the ones in the north, the countryside becomes more picturesque.

Continue along the N6 to Chalon-sur-Saône.

Lunch at Chalon-sur-Saône.

Although a crossroads of important highways, a rail junction and a river port at the confluence of the Saône and Canal du Centre, Chalon appears as a gracious tranquil town and is a pleasant stopping place. Seats beside the sleepy greeny-yellow Saône give it the atmosphere of a quiet holiday resort. Grande Rue runs through the old town, which incidentally dates back to pre-Roman times, when it was a centre for the Eduens.

Visit its cathedral, St Vincent, first erected in the 5th century on a pagan temple then rebuilt from the 11th to the 15th century. To note are some of the old capitals, a tapestry dating from 1510 and its cloister. A museum worth seeing is Musée Denon, beside the Town Hall. It was named after Vivant Denon, the Director General of museums in France in 1802. It contains a very good collection of pre-historic flint instruments from south-west Burgundy, paintings and sculpture, antique and medieval articles, etc.

Nicéphore Niepce (1765-1833), pioneer of photography, came from here. You will see his statue standing in Place du Port. Nearby is a museum devoted to his simple experiments. In 1822 he succeeded in fixing an image previously obtained in the dark room on a glass plate. Thus you could call him the father of photography. Niepce worked for long hours and at great expense on projects which brought him very little money. He went into partnership with Daguerre in 1829 but died, alas, in 1833, when he was just about to be successful.

As you are now near the river, you could cross Pont St Laurent to the island. Here to see is the 16th-century hospital, particularly its refectory, and the 15th-century Tour du Doyenne (it once belonged to the cathedral but has been re-erected here). Climb to its summit!

Follow the N6 to Tournus.

Mâconnais

Mâconnais, which is a succession of small hills, stretches for about 35 kms along the west side of the Saône and links the noble aristocratic vineyards of the Côte d'Or with the humbler Beaujolais. The soil is chiefly calcareous and its most celebrated wine is Pouilly-Fuissé. Lesser-known but of the same family are Pouilly-Loché and Pouilly-Vinzelles. The red wines here, although not great, are good value.

Tournus

Tournus, situated on the west bank of the Saône at the northern end of the Mâconnais, lies in a region of good stone and wine. Delightful old houses, cobbled streets and several reputable restaurants, make it a good place to stop.

Its abbey church, St Philibert, dating from the 10th century and dominating the town from every angle, is one of the most grandiose and best-preserved Romanesque buildings in France. It has an unusual, sober, almost military purity, more reminiscent of a castle than a church.

St Valerian was martyred at Tournus at the end of the 2nd century and pilgrimages to his tomb led to the foundation of a monastery by Charles the Bald in 875 AD. This was destroyed during the Hungarian invasion of 937 but, when it was rebuilt, it also sheltered the remains of St Philibert, a Gascon, who founded two important 7th-century abbeys. St Valerian's relics still retain the place of honour in the church and the annual pilgrimage here is for both saints.

Tournus has two museums worth seeing. Musée Perrins de Puycousin, facing St Philibert, is in a 17th-century house. Wax models in regional costumes show how local people lived and worked. The Musée Greuse in Rue de Colleeg is devoted to Jean Baptiste Greuze (1725-1805), born in Tournus of an artisan family. Some original paintings, engravings and drawings and a few personal mementoes help to bring to life a man whose artistic career went well, then badly. His somewhat surgary romantic style went out of favour after the Revolution.

Detour

Take the D14 from Tournus to Brancion.

Brancion, prettily sited on a rocky spur between two ravines, once commanded the pass linking Tournus to the Grosne valley and was the seat of a powerful barony. Some of its strategically-placed defences remain, such as its ramparts and the château (founded in the 10th century), which dominates the narrow streets. An account of how Jocemand de Brancion met his death fighting beside St Louis (France's saintly king, Louis IX) at the battle of Mansourah (1250) is inscribed above the fireplace in the château's big hall. There is a good view of the village and Grosne valley from the top of the keep. The church, St Pierre, is a masterpiece of late Romanesque art: its pure lines are visible from a great distance. It contains some remarkable 14th-century frescoes and the effigy of the recumbent figure of Jocemand de Brancion on a tomb.

You could continue through the woods, to Chapaize, whose church's tall rectangular Romanesque bell tower (35 metres), a landmark for miles, crowns the village. It was here that Bénédictine novices of Chalon had their abbey house. St Martin's church (11th- to 12th-century), restored, has a stern grandeur.

Further on still stands the beautiful 17th-century château Cormatin, birthplace of novelist Jacques Lacretelle. Built in 1605, it is France's best château in which to see how the nobility lived in Louis XIII's time. You can examine everything from grounds to kitchen to bedrooms. Its decor is exceptionally rich and rooms contain magnificent furniture and paintings and tapestries, in marked contrast with the rather sober but elegant architecture.

Return to Tournus (D981/215).

Overnight at Tournus.

Le Bourgogne
28 Rue Strasbourg
71100 Chalon-sur-Saône
Tel: (85) 48 89 18

You can either eat in the formal restaurant or the 13th-century cellars. The chef/patron concentrates on local and regional dishes.

Closed:	Sunday evenings in winter
Credit cards:	Carte Bleu, Euro
Food:	Regional
Rating:	★★★

TOURNUS: USEFUL INFORMATION

Tourist Office:	Place Carnot
	Tel: (85) 51 13 10
Population:	6,704
General Interest:	Ancient abbey and church

Hôtel de Greuze
5 le Place de l'Abbaye
71700 Tournus
Tel: (85) 40 77 77

A chic and elegant hotel. The accommodation is on the expensive side, but it is possible to eat very reasonably from the 'menu touristique'.

Closed:	Open all year
Rooms:	21
Facilities:	Minibars and bathrooms with all rooms plus television and video
Credit cards:	Carte Bleu, Am.Ex, Diners
Food:	Try Quenelles de Brochet Nantua and Pâté en croûte
Rating:	★★★★

69

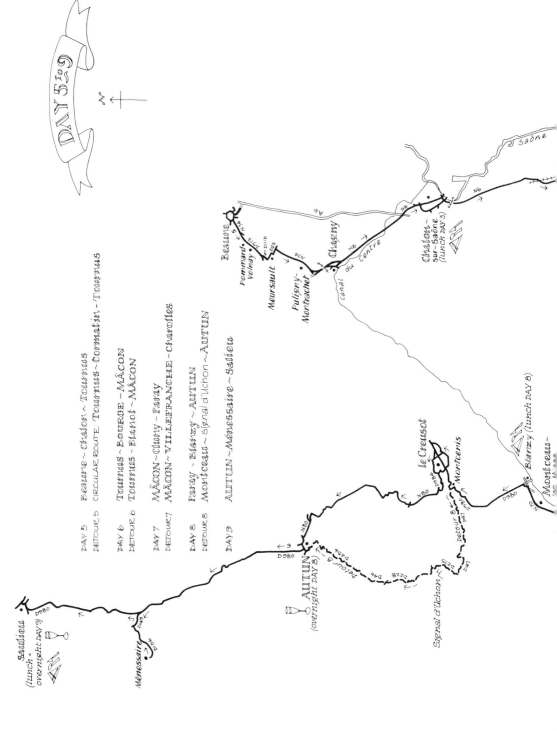

DAY 5 to 9

DAY 5   Beaune ~ Chalon ~ Tournus
DETOUR 5   CIRCULAR ROUTE: Tournus ~ Cormatin ~ Tournus

DAY 6   Tournus ~ Bourge ~ Mâcon
DETOUR 6   Tournus ~ Blanot ~ Mâcon

DAY 7   Mâcon ~ Cluny ~ Paray
DETOUR 7   Mâcon ~ Villefranche ~ Charolles

DAY 8   Paray ~ Blanzy ~ Autun
DETOUR 8   Montceau ~ Signal d'Uchon ~ Autun

DAY 9   Autun ~ Ménessaire ~ Saulieu

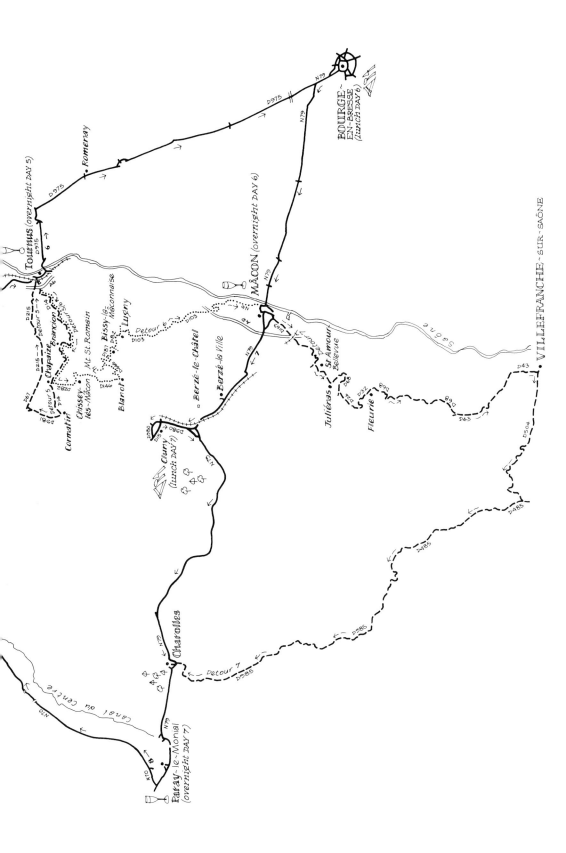

DAY 6

Tournus, Bourg-en-Bresse, Mâcon: approx. 93 km (58 miles)

The main route goes through fortified Romenay to Bourg-en-Bresse (with delightful old quarter) for lunch and then westwards to Mâcon — which welcomes all gourmets. Alternatively you could omit Bourg-en-Bresse and follow the hills and villages of the Mâconnais — one of the most picturesque areas in Burgundy — into Mâcon.

Overnight at Mâcon.

Map references

Tournus	4°55′E 46°34′N
Romenay	5°04′E 46°30′N
Bourg-en-Bresse	5°14′E 46°13′N
Mâcon	4°50′E 46°19′N

Detour

Brancion	4°48′E 46°33′N
Chapaize	4°44′E 46°34′N
Chissey-lès-Mâcons	4°44′E 46°32′N
Mont St Romain	4°45′E 46°30′N
Blanot	4°44′E 46°28′N
Bissy	4°47′E 46°28′N
Lugny	4°48′E 46°27′N

Route shown p. 71.

Verdun-sur-le-Doubs

Travels in Burgundy

Breakfast at Tournus.

Depart Tournus.

Take the D975 to Bourg-en-Bresse, passing the old fortified town of Romenay (note 14th-century half-timbered houses along the main street, east and west town gates still standing).

Bourg-en-Bresse

Bourg, a busy agricultural and business centre, situated on the flat Bresse plain, is chiefly noted for its Brou — a small village, now part of the town's outskirts — clustered around a Bénédictine priory on the N75.

The church and monastery were built as a result of a vow made by Margaret of Bourbon who promised to transform the humble priory of Brou into a monastery if her husband, Philip, Count of Bresse, recovered from a hunting accident. He did, but she herself died before she could fulfil the vow, which was finally fulfilled by her daughter-in-law, another Margaret. When her own husband, Philibert, died suddenly she saw this as a punishment for the unfulfilled vow.

Margaret of Austria, who was living in Flanders, entrusted the building of the church and fabulous shrine to a Flemish master-mason, Van Boghem, who succeeded in erecting the building in nineteen years (1513-1532) but its completion came two years after Margaret's own death.

The monastery has had a varied career. It escaped the ravages of the Wars of Religion and the Revolution, but it has been a pig-sty, a barracks, a paupers' home and lunatic asylum. In 1823, it was turned into a seminary, and now houses the Musée de l'Ain.

It is well worth a visit, as is most certainly the grand and spacious church with its lofty white pillars, nave, choir and stalls, typical of the French Renaissance and a monument to a historic marriage. The carvings are exquisite — beautiful, intricate and delicate. Philibert lies in the centre of the grand chamber — a prone white statue on a black marble slab, angels at his head, sword by his side, feet resting on a young lion (emblem of strength). Bourbon Margaret of Burgundy lies on one side, Margaret of Austria on the other, a dog (symbol of fidelity), at both their feet. A German, Conrad Meyt, trained in Flanders, was responsible for the three princely effigies in carrara marble, while the ornamentation and smaller statuary were done by French, Italian and German assistants in a Flemish workshop set up in Brou. The windows of the choir were the work of a local studio.

The old quarter of Bourg has some well-preserved 15th- and 16th-century houses. Note particularly Rue Victor Basch and the Rue du Palais.

Lunch at Bourg-en-Bresse.

N79 to Mâcon.

Mâcon

Like Chalon-sur-Saône, the best part of Mâcon lies beside the broad Saône, whose gardens alongside put one in mind of the seaside. Unfortunately here a noisy stream of traffic rather detracts from its peacefulness.

In Roman times the town was known as Matisco and it was later the seat of a powerful medieval county. Today's busy wine trading centre is not particularly attractive, but as it lies at a crossroads of highways and is noted for its good food and wine, it makes an ideal stopping place for a gourmet travelling along the wine road.

Mâcon was the birthplace of Alphonse de Lamartine (1790-1869), so you will see much around the town to remind you of him and his work. There is a Quai Lamartine; while a statue to him stands nearby on the Promenade Lamartine. Hôtel Senecé, an 18th-century architectural jewel, became the property of the Art, Science and Writing Academy in Mâcon: Lamartine was several times its president. It now holds the Lamartine museum, exhibiting documents and souvenirs from the poet's life. There is even a Lamartine circuit (about 64 kms) which takes in some of the places which inspired his verse.

Mâcon also boasts a Hôtel Dieu, built in the 18th century, which has an interesting pharmacy with a beautiful collection of pots. The municipal museum is housed in the old convent of the Ursulines, founded to educate young girls from the nobility and middle classes. During the Revolution — feelings ran high here — it became the town's most important jail. Lamartine's father was incarcerated here during the Terror. On the ground floor is the department of archaeology and pre-history. Information about the famous Solutré rock, which has given its name to an archaeological period and is about 15 kms to the west of the town (there is a museum there), is carefully recorded and explained. The first floor is devoted to various aspects of local life; the second and third floor to paintings and engravings.

Carnot street, a main shopping boulevard, has always been important, although it used to be called Bourg Neuf. Notice the Poor Home, La Charité, or Résidence Soufflot, recently restored. It was built due to the good offices of St Vincent de Paul, friend of the poor, but was only completed in 1762. Abandoned children would be left here. A poor woman would put the baby in a sort of swivelling barrel and then ring the home's bell. A nun would come out at once and collect the child. It is now an old people's home.

Don't miss Maison de Bois (1490-1510) at the corner of Place aux Herbes, off rue Dombey. Its wooden front, which has been compared to a wooden chest, is decorated with cheeky statues (satyrs, monsters and animals). The house was supposed to have belonged to a wine-drinking group of masons, who were banned after a scandal in 1625.

Off the N6 on the banks of the Saône stands the highly reputable Maison Mâçonnais des Vins. Opened in 1958 to promote the local wines, this offers much more than just another taste before you buy. Here you can eat a full meal of local specialities, accompanied at each stage by the appropriate wines. The cellars hold 20 of the local appellations — Beaujolais, Mâçonnais and Chalonnais. Thus a visit here summarises much that has been seen and tasted over the last few days.

Detour

If you take the winding scenic route from Tournus to Mâcon, you will pass through one of the most attractive regions in Burgundy. This is a gentle hospitable countryside, not grand but picturesque on a small scale, and probably contains more Romanesque village churches than anywhere else in Europe.

Follow the D14 to Brancion and Chapaize (see p. 68) and continue south to Chissey-lès-Mâcons (D282), the site of a Gallo-Roman villa and later the kings of France came here to hunt. The village lies in the valley at the foot of Mont St Romain. Skirting the mountains head for Blanot (D146), a tiny village surrounding a simple square-towered 11th-century church. During the summer here you can visit some underground caves (Grottes-Gouffre de Blanot). Follow the D446 toward the summit of Mont St Romain. There is a road to take you to the top which, on a clear day, offers a stunning view from the Alps across to the Morvan (p. 101) in the west. Continue westwards (D187/82) through Bissy to Lugny — note spectacular view of vineyards from St Pierre wine tasting centre — and then take the D103 winding gradually into Mâcon.

Dinner and overnight at Mâcon.

Auberge Bressane
166 Boulevard de Brou
01000 Bourg-en-Bresse
Tel: (74) 22 22 68

Opposite the Eglise de Brou, one of the main sights of the town, this pretty flower-filled restaurant serves smart food and is extremely proud of its extensive wine list.

Closed:	Closed Monday evenings and Tuesdays
Credit cards:	Diners, Visa, Am.Ex
Food:	Seasonal specialities with emphasis on local traditions.
Rating:	★★★★

Le Savoie
15 Rue P. Pioda
01000 Bourg-en-Bresse
Tel: (74) 23 29 24

Closed:	16 July-13 August, 26 December-2 January, Wednesday evenings and Saturdays
Credit cards:	Am.Ex, Diners, Visa, Euro
Food:	Good value and high standard
Rating:	★★

BOURG-EN-BRESSE: USEFUL INFORMATION

Tourist Office:		6 Ave Alsace-Lorraine
		Tel: (74) 22 49 40
	and	(June-September)
		168 Boulevard de Brou
		Tel: (74) 22 27 76
Population:		43,675
General Interest:		Ancient churches, the Brou, museum

Hôtel Terminus
91 Rue Victor Hugo
71000 Mâcon
Tel: (85) 39 17 11

A large modern hotel with full facilities at surprisingly modest rates. A selection of menus is offered by the enthusiastic chef, M. Bevas, which includes a gastronomic menu with 6 or 7 choices for each course at a bargain price.

Closed:	Open all year
Rooms:	53
Facilities:	Television in all rooms, telephone direct, garage, piano bar, restaurant

Credit cards: Am.Ex, Diners, Visa, Euro
Food: Try their Saumon au choux or
     Filet de Boeuf avec sauce
     échalotte
Rating: ★★★

Hôtel Bellevue
416-20 Quai Lamartine
71000 Mâcon
Tel: (85) 38 05 07

Closed: Open all year
Rooms: 25
Facilities: Television, restaurant
Credit cards: Carte Bleu, Am.Ex, Diners, Euro
Rating: ★★★

MÂCON: USEFUL INFORMATION

Tourist Office:	187 Rue Carnot
	Tel: (85) 39 71 37
Population:	38,719
Facilities:	Golf course (7 km)
General Interest:	Museum, old buildings, wine tasting

DAY 7

Mâcon, Cluny, Charolles, Paray-le-Monial: approx. 77 km (48 miles)

The morning is spend at Cluny; for centuries this abbey's power was felt throughout Europe. But its destruction was such that its remnants have to be hunted out amid the little town of Cluny. After lunch we cross to the cattle town of Charolles before reaching Paray-le-Monial, with its famous Basilica, centre of pilgrimages to the Sacred Heart.

Overnight at Paray-le-Monial.

Map references
Mâcon	4°50'E 46°19'N
Berzé-la-Ville	4°43'E 46°22'N
Berzé-le-Châtel	4°42'E 46°23'N
Cluny	4°39'E 46°26'N
Charolles	4°17'E 46°26'N
Paray-le-Monial	4°07'E 46°27'N

Detour
St-Amour	4°45'E 46°15'N
Juliénas	4°44'E 46°14'N
Fleurie	4°42'E 46°12'N
Villié-Morgon	4°41'E 46°10'N
Cercié	4°40'E 46°07'N
Le Perrèon	4°36'E 46°04'N
Vaux	4°35'E 46°04'N
Villefranche	4°44'E 45°59'N

Route shown p. 71.

Cluny, street scene

Travels in Burgundy

Breakfast at Mâcon.

Leave Mâcon on the N79, D980 to Cluny.

Berzé-la-Ville

On this route you will pass Berzé-la-Ville, once the residence of the Abbots of Cluny. The small chapel, St Hugh, attached to their priory, managed to escape the 12th-century fire there. In 1887 some magnificent Romanesque frescoes, representing Christ in majesty, the death of St Blaize and the martyrdom of St Vincent were discovered beneath a coating of distemper. They are reckoned to be the largest Romanesque paintings to have survived from Cluny. Then, on a high slope among vineyards, looms Berzé-le-Châtel, quite well-preserved, the castle which protected the southern approaches to the great abbey.

Cluny

You will need to use your imagination when visiting today's Cluny. Incorporated in the town are the tower of the church, remains of the Romanesque abbey, claustral buildings, gardens and flour store. Plans and models in the Musée Ochier, situated in the Abbot's palace, are really all that exist to show you what Cluny must have looked like in the days of its glory. I recommend first a visit to the Musée Ochier. Its collections of paintings, sculptures, gothic chests, intricate stonework and vast library combine to display something of the grandeur of Cluny and these, as well as the models, will help you to discern the traces when exploring the town. From the centre of Cluny, there is a good panoramic view over the town from the Tour des Fromages (11th-century).

Cluny abbey was founded in 910 by William the Pious, Count of Mâcon, with Berno, its Abbot and twelve monks, who wanted to live in solitude and prayer away from the world. Its expansion was extraordinarily rapid. By the 12th century, Cluny had become so large and wealthy that it was a powerful state on its own, owing allegiance only to the Pope. Its learned abbots were more statesmen than men of the church. Kings came to them for counsel. The abbots lived and entertained in royal style. There were Cluniac dependencies in Italy, Germany, England, Poland, Switzerland and Spain, with more than 10,000 monks under its authority. However, many deplored the luxurious way in which the monks lived and as early as 1098 another monastery was founded at Cîteaux, whose white-robed monks were known as Cistercians. Their very strict rule, later reinforced by the young nobleman, St Bernard, who had renounced his riches, became a powerful influence (see p. 60).

Cluny gradually fell from power. It was sacked by the Huguenots in 1562, and lost much of its prestige during the time of Cardinals Mazarin and Richelieu. Even so, it was still considered a symbol of the hated order by the Revolutionaries, and in 1793 — it had been closed down in 1790 — it was attacked by the mob. Pictures, papers and books were burned. Women cut up the gold and silver fabrics they found there for dress materials. The great bell was taken down to be melted for cannon for the army. In 1798, the abbey was put up for sale and the new owner, a merchant from Mâcon, demolished the nave. Further mutilations followed. By 1823, nothing remained but ruins of what had once been the most powerful church in Christendom.

However, it is an important tourist centre and the town has other objects of interest, such as a beautiful monumental gate (once the entrance to the abbey); houses from various periods along Rue de la République; the Hôtel Dieu; various old churches; promenades and a National Horse Stud Farm.

Lunch at Cluny.

Detour

As an alternative to Cluny, some people might like to visit the Beaujolais region.

The name Beaujolais comes from Beaujeu, the name of a powerful family in the 12th and 13th centuries. The region, an approx. 64 kms strip on the west side of the road between Mâcon and Lyon, is generally considered to be outside Burgundy. Its landscape — high hills dotted with woods, pleasant valleys and roads meandering past vineyards — is popular for touring. The village of Vaux-en-Beaujolais in the centre of vineyards was the model for Gabriel Chevalier's amusing novel, *Clochemerle*. Beaujolais wines are particularly popular in France, where they are drunk under various names. Unlike Burgundian wine it should be drunk cool and very young — so young, in fact, that some is flown to London wine-bars and shops almost as soon as the season is declared open. The following names call for attention — Moulin à Vent, Fleurie Saint-Amour, Chiroubles, Morgon, Julienas, Brouilly, Chenas and Côte de Brouilly.

Villefranche-sur-Saône, industrial and commercial, capital of the Beaujolais since 1532, can be reached from Mâcon, either by the mountain route, about 97 kms, or by the vineyards (via Saint-Amour, Juliénas, Fleurie, Villié-Morgon, Cercié, Le Perréon and Vaux) about 50 kms (plenty of wine-tasting). Both ways are attractive. Otherwise take N6, the journey is about 37 kms.

Charolles can be reached from Villefranche, crossing the Beaujolais, east to west, D504/485/985.

From Cluny take the D980/N79 to Charolles.

Charolles

Charolles, a pleasant little town encircled by the Arconce and the Semence rivers, lies at the heart of a lush countryside. It is a cattle-breeding country and the original home of the Charolais, those herds of white beasts you will have seen browsing over the fields during your travels through Burgundy. Large farms, resembling ranches, have given the region the nickname *The Far West*.

The Charolais breed was created fairly recently. In size, only Norman cattle are larger; in quality, they are second to none and are now imported to improve breeding-stocks in countries as far away as Argentina. If here on a Thursday, you might like to visit the picturesque Charolais cattle-market at nearby Saint-Christophe-en-Brionnais (8 a.m.). You can also eat pot-au-feu (stew) and entrecôte in the surrounding inns.

Charolles, capital of the Charollais, is dominated by its ruined château, which changed hands many times. Its tower, in the Town Hall garden, and from which there are some good views, bears the name Charles the Rash, perhaps its most famous owner. Since 1845 the town has had a faïence industry. The René Davoine museum has displays of sculpture (stone, wood and marble). On the first Saturday and Sunday of August (odd years only), Charolles holds an important festival of folklore.

Take N79 to Paray-le-Monial.

Paray-le-Monial

Paray-le-Monial, well sited beside the river Bourbince and Canal du Centre, lies between the Charollais and Brionnais districts. A mile before the town lies the

Château of Cypierre. An imposing structure with a huge dungeon — it was built over an ancient defence post on the Roman road to Autun. Like Lourdes, Paray is a popular centre for pilgrims and gets crowded in summer. So it is advisable to book ahead. Its famous basilica of the Sacred Heart (first known as Notre-Dame and restored in the 19th and 20th centuries) was built at the same time as Cluny and has been described.as a pocket-sized edition of what once stood there.

The Worship of the Sacred Heart dates from 1673 when a nun, Sister Marguerite-Marie Lacoque, had a succession of visitations. She claimed that Christ visited her and charged her to advocate the worship of the Sacred Heart which 'so loved mankind'. She died in 1690, aged 43. The visitation convent was confiscated during the Revolution and the Worship of the Sacred Heart did not gather momentum again until the beginning of the 19th century. She was beatified in 1864 and canonised in 1920. A great pilgrimage to Paray-la-Monial took place in 1873 (Sacré Coeur in Montmartre, Paris, was started a few years later, an atonement for the Franco-Prussian war). Since then pilgrimages have been made here every year. The Magnificat, an event to celebrate the arts, whose main inspiration and important patron was the church, takes place from 8-12 July. Artists, dancers, musicians, actors, singers and sculptors take part.

Close to the Basilica de Sacré Coeur is the Sanctuaire des Apparitions where Sister Marguerite-Marie had her principal revelations and where her body is preserved in a gilt and silver shrine, and the Chambres des Reliques in the house of the Pages of Cardinal Bouillon, where many souvenirs have been preserved and her cell reconstructed. The Musée de Hiéron on the northern outskirts of the town is worth a visit. It is devoted to the Eucharist theme and also contains paintings by Tiepolo, Mignard and Lebrun and has an exceptionally fine tympanum.

Note also the Renaissance facade of the Hôtel de Ville and the 16th-century Tower of St Nicholas.

Dinner and overnight at Paray-le-Monial.

Hôtel Bourgogne
Place Abbaye
Cluny
Tel: (85) 89 00 58

Right opposite the ruins of the Abbey the restaurant of this hotel offers top quality food.

Closed:	15 November to 15 February, Wednesday and Thursday lunchtimes
Rooms:	14
Facilities:	Garage
Credit cards:	Euro, Visa, Diners, Am.Ex.
Food:	Their specialities include Rôti de lotte aux pommes appétit and Canette de Barbarie aux baies roses
Rating:	★★★★

CLUNY: USEFUL INFORMATION

Tourist Office:	6 Rue Mercière Tel: (85) 59 05 34
Population:	4,734
General Interest:	Abbey remains, museum.

Les Trois Pigeons
2 Rue Dargaud
71600 Paray-le-Monial
Tel: (85) 81 03 77

A good value hotel with bedrooms in a range of prices. Pleasant, straightforward bar and restaurant. The menu prices match the bedrooms. If required you could spend the night here very economically and happily if your budget is suffering from some of the other more luxurious establishments en route.

Closed:	1 December-1 March
Rooms:	47
Facilities:	Two rooms accessible to handicapped guests
Credit cards:	Carte Bleu, Am.Ex, Mastercard
Food:	Good value
Rating:	★★

Aux Vendanges de Bourgogne
5 Rue Denis-Papin
71600 Paray-le-Monial
Tel: (85) 81 13 43

Closed:	January to March
Rooms:	14
Facilities:	Television in the bar
Credit cards:	Carte Bleu, Am.Ex
Food:	Their specialities — Coq au Beaujolais, Le canard à l'orange, Le filet charollais grillé au feu du bois
Rating:	★★

PARAY-LE-MONIAL: USEFUL INFORMATION

Tourist Ofice:	Ave Jean-Paul II
	Tel: (85) 81 10 92
Population:	11,312
General Interest:	Old buildings, basilica, museum

Autun

DAY 8

Paray-le-Monial, Montceau-les-Mines, Le Creusot, Autun: approx. 86 kms (54 miles)

Head north into the industrial centre around Le Creusot — an interesting place to visit, contrasting well with the side of Burgundy you have so far seen on the trip. Beyond lies Autun, a tranquil relaxed old town on the edge of the Morvan.

Map references
Paray-le-Monial	4°07'E 46°27'N
Montceau-les-Mines	4°22'E 46°42'N
Le Creusot	4°25'E 46°48'N
Autun	4°18'E 46°57'N

Detour
Montcenis	4°23'E 46°47'N
Signal d'Uchon	4°15'E 46°48'N

Route shown p. 71.

Breakfast at Paray-le-Monial.

Depart Paray-le-Monial on the N70 to Montceau-les-Mines.

Montceau-les-Mines

Montceau-les-Mines, crossed by the Canal du Centre, is an industrial town which grew up in the vicinity of the mining village of Blanzy. It has two museums: one a primary school museum, which shows two classrooms, one from 1881-1925, the other from 1925-1960, which tell the story of education from the time of Jules Ferry: the other is a geological museum, a permanent exhibition of fossils found in the surrounding coal-mining area. At Mont-St-Vincent, D970 (11 kms away), is an archæological museum, showing 'digs' from the region: it is housed in an old salt warehouse.

Continue on the D980 to Montcenis, and D984 to Le Creusot.

Le Creusot

You are now well and truly in the industrial area of Burgundy. Although coal was found round here in the 16th century its mining was done in a haphazard way and it was not until about a century later, when large deposits had been discovered, that it was used to fire iron ore. By the time of the Revolution there was a foundry and glassworks at Le Creusot. The manufacture of cristaux (glass) de la reine Marie-Antoinette was transferred here from Sévrès in 1787. In 1794 the Canal du Centre opened linking the region by water through to Paris and Lyon. Thus the products could be shipped direct to the main markets.

The industries declined after the fall of Napoleon, but in 1836, Joseph Eugene Schneider and his brother Adolphe bought them and set themselves up in Le Creusot, then a very small town. They began to build steam locomotives and steam engines for ships. Then in 1841, a M. Bourdon, one of their engineers, invented the power hammer, which enabled heavy castings to be made. From then onwards, the factories could produce equipment for great power stations, ports and mines.

The Schneider family were benefactors as well as entrepreneurs. They built schools, hospitals and churches and shaped the community that stretched from Montceau to Blanzy. You will see many statues to them around the town, as well as the monument to the power hammer.

In fact, this so-called industrial town is quite a pleasant place to visit, with its large central park, artificial lakes, a hill walk, but not forgetting the large power-hammer (21 metres high), the source of its wealth, and which dominates the eastern entrance to the town.

Chiefly to see here is the Queen Marie-Antoinette Crystal Glassworks in the château de la Verrière, once the residence of the Schneider family. Outside stand two enormous kilns. One has been turned into a theatre; the other is used for exhibitions. As in parts of Britain now, industrial tourism has become a feature of this type of town, and there are guided tours, lasting from one to several days of Le Creusot, the factory town; a tour of the coal mines of Montceau-les-Mines; daily tours around the Ecomuseum (about the urban community), and daily tours of the canal and its industries.

Lunch at Le Creusot or Montceau-les-Mines

Follow the D984/N80 to Autun.

Detour

For a more scenic route from Montcenis to Autun take D47/275/228/46/256, via the village and Signal d'Uchon (681 ms). This is a desolate mountain top with boulders and strange-shaped rocks, many of which, such as the 'Devil's Claw' and

The Devil's Claw

91

the 'Tottering stone' have eerie legends attached to them. Botanists, geologists and mycologists enjoy exploring its treasures. You would perhaps be more interested in the magnificent view over the Morvan and Côte d'Or from its summit.

Autun

Autun, originally called Augustodunum, was founded by the Emperor Augustus, who used it as a base to hold down and subdue the rebellious Eduens. Its good position on the road between Lyon and Boulogne brought it such prosperity that it even rivalled Rome. Unfortunately, subsequent invasions and pillagings have destroyed many of its old buildings. There are now only two gateways and the ruins of a theatre, and a temple on its outskirts to remind one of this era.

Today's Autun is a tranquil timeless old town, backed by wooded hills. Its cathedral St Lazare (built 1120-1146) boasts a tympanum (above centre door), representing the Last Judgement (work of Gislebertus) which is one of the most magnificent in France. A huge Christ is surrounded by smaller angels, three zodiacs and terrified devils. St Lazare, built to house the precious remains of St Lazarus, friend of Jesus (brought to Marseilles by Gérard de Roussillion) replaced an earlier cathedral dedicated to St Nazaire. Its exterior has lost its Romanesque character — belfry and tall spire (built by Cardinal Rolin after a storm had destroyed the tower) date from the end of the 15th century. Two towers over the doorway date from the last century. Inside to note are the capitals. You will need a plan to study them in their fascinating detail. They represent episodes from the Bible and from church and French history.

Nearby is Musée Rolin, situated in part of the 15th-century mansion of Chancellor Rolin, who founded Hôtel Dieu in Beaune. One of his sons was Cardinal Rolin, who became Bishop of Autun, and was responsible for the town becoming an important religious centre. To see here are Gallo-Roman antiquities, (including items excavated from Mont Beuvray, p. 110), statuary from St Lazare 15th- and 16th-century paintings and sculpture and souvenirs of the Rolin family.

The remains of the Roman amphitheatre lies to the south of Port André. It once housed 15,000 spectators, who came here to watch wild beast and gladiatorial contests. In summer the amphitheatre is used for a massive historical pageant of Autun's history, performed by a cast of about 600. Check with the Tourist

Office for performance dates — in such a setting the spectacle should be quite tremendous.

Autun is a good centre for explorations, especially into the rugged wooded Morvan. When here try and find time to visit the château at Sully, about 5 kms away (D975/326). This magnificent ensemble, a mixture of fantasy and sobriety, was described by Madame de Sévigné is the Fontainebleau of Burgundy. The original château, a medieval fortress, belonging to the Bishops of Autun, was replaced by Gaspard de Tavannes in 1515. Fortunately it managed to escape confiscation and destruction during the Revolution.

The building is approached by an avenue of box-shaped bushes. Its moat is crossed by a five-arched bridge. One of its best features is the great staircase which leads from the centre of the north wing to a semicircular terrace, overlooking an ornamental lake. Only the exterior grounds and servants quarters are open to the public.

Dinner and overnight at Autun.

'La France' Hôtel Restaurant

7 Place Beaubernard
71800 Montceau-les-Mines
Tel: (85) 57 26 64

A small hotel run by the proprietor and chef Paul Chouin.

Closed:	August and Mondays
Credit cards:	Carte Bleu, Euro, Mastercard
Food:	Charollais meat a speciality
Rating:	★★

La Vieux Saule

Torcy
Tel: (85) 55 09 53

4 km out of Le Creusot this restaurant serves very good food. You can dine outside if the weather is fine.

Closed:	Sunday evenings and Mondays
Credit cards:	Euro, Visa
Ratings:	★★★

Hôtel St Louis

6 Rue de l'Arbalete
71400 Autun
Tel: (85) 52 21 03

This is the grand hotel of the town with atmosphere to match. Both the room charge and the fixed price menu are extremely reasonable but you could go to town on the à la carte menu in the elegant La Rotunda restaurant.

Closed:	20 December-2 February, Sunday evenings and Mondays

Rooms:	52
Credit cards:	Carte Bleu, Am.Ex, Visa, Diners
Food:	sauté de Boeuf à la Bourguignon
Rating:	★★★

For a gourmet meal:

Le Chalet Bleu
3 Rue Jeanin
71400 Autun
Tel: (85) 86 27 30

The à la carte menu at this establishment will appeal to true food buffs. It includes such unusual dishes as Snail ravioli with garden herbs and Supreme of guinea fowl with foie gras and pear fondue. Other dishes however appeal to more straightforward tastes.

Closed:	Monday evenings and Tuesdays
Credit cards:	Carte Bleu, Am.Ex, Diners
Rating:	★★★

AUTUN: USEFUL INFORMATION

Tourist Office:	Ave Charles de Gaulle
	Tel: (85) 52 20 34
Population:	16,320
General Interest:	Cathedral, old buildings, museum, Château de Sully (15 km)

DAY 9

Autun, Ménessaire, Saulieu: approx. 52 km (33 miles)

Today is destined to be a relaxing day enjoying the food of the area. Both Autun and Saulieu are blessed with excellent restaurants and you may choose to lunch in either. However do allow yourself time to visit Saulieu's museum where the exhibition will do much to prepare you for visiting the Morvan tomorrow.

Overnight at Saulieu.

Map references
Autun   4°18'E 46°57'N
Ménessaire   4°08'E 47°08'N
Saulieu   4°14'E 47°17'N

Route shown p. 71.

Château de Sully

Breakfast at Autun.

You can either spend the morning in Autun and lunch there before heading north to Saulieu, or leave Autun in time to reach Saulieu for lunch. Given the high standard of restaurants in both towns, the choice could be difficult.

Depart Autun taking the D980 to Saulieu. A turning off the route north along the D149/D106 leads through woodland to Ménessaire, a medieval château with traditional multi-coloured Burgundian roofs. From here you can look out across the Morvan or back eastwards to the gentler Côte d'Or through which you have travelled.

Saulieu

Saulieu, on the Morvan's eastern edge, is a town long famous for its hospitality and good food. It is a good place to spend a restful day. During the 17th century, it was a favourite stopping-place for travellers between Paris and Lyon. Now, situated at a crossroads of many main roads, it makes a very good centre for exploring the Naturel Régional Parc du Morvan.

Saulieu's name is probably derived from the Roman Sidolocus, which stood on the main route to the south. Three Christian missionaries from Autun, St Andoche, St Thyrse and St Felix, were martyred here and the famous Romanesque basilica, St Andoche, is named after one of them. Maybe you should visit it before wining and dining at Saulieu. Even the virtuous Madame de Sévigné found herself the worse for drink after a lavish meal here on her way to Vichy in 1677. In atonement, she presented the basilica with a statue of the Virgin (it has de Sévigné's face). You can see it in the north aisle.

St Andoche's main features are its sculptured capitals, which depict mostly very realistic floral themes. Five are from the Bible — the Flight into Egypt, the Temptation of Christ, Balaam and his ass, the suicide of Judas, and Christ meeting Mary Magdalene after the Resurrection.

In the 5th century a tomb was erected over the bodies of the three dead martyrs and the monastic community that settled here drew many pilgrims to the town, among them Charlemagne himself. A basilica was built, then rebuilt by Charlemagne after it had been destroyed by Saracen invaders. The church was consecrated in 1119. It suffered during the Hundred Years' War, then was restored and added to. Its church was rebuilt in the 18th century and the steeple placed on the north tower was crowned with an Italian dome. The facade of St Andoche is uninspiring, but don't miss a view of the marble sarcophagus to St Andoche in the north transept.

After the church you can visit the museum next door (archaeology, local and regional history, Gallo-Roman steles, a Morvan kitchen and rural crafts including examples of the local tanning industry). It also contains the work of animal sculptor, François Pompon (1853-1933) who was born here. When apprenticed to a marble-cutter in Paris, he would often slip away to visit the Jardin des Plantes to study the ways the animals moved in the zoo. You can see his bull standing in a flowery square near the N6 entrance to the town. The museum is housed in what was the presbytery (17th-century).

A succession of famous chefs have placed Saulieu's Côte d'Or among the best restaurants in France.

Dinner and overnight at Saulieu.

SAULIEU: USEFUL INFORMATION

Tourist Office:	Rue d'Argentine
	Tel: (80) 64 00 21
Population:	3,183

Le Côte d'Or
2 Rue d'Argentine
Saulieu
Tel: (80) 64 07 66

This hotel is a member of the Relais and Chateaux Group and its décor is truly gracious and elegant. There is a beautiful walled garden where breakfast can be served on the terrace. Although a few of the rooms are modestly priced, depending on the booking situation you may be obliged to accept a larger and more expensive room.

Closed:	Open all year
Rooms:	15 + 9 apartments
Facilities:	Televisions in rooms, car parking
Credit cards:	Carte Bleu, Am.Ex, Euro, Diners
Food:	Cooking is of top standard (and prices reflect this). Try their speciality — Frogs legs with garlic purée.
Rating:	★★★★

Alternatively, a very small hotel:

Hôtel Borne Imperiale
14-16 Rue d'Argentine
21200 Saulieu
Tel: (80) 64 19 76

Closed:	31 October-1 December and Wednesdays
Rooms:	7
Facilities:	Television in rooms, restaurant
Credit cards:	Carte Bleu
Rating:	★★

DAY 10

Saulieu, St Brisson, Quarré-les-Tombes, Château-Chinon: approx. 100 kms (63 miles)

Today's tour weaves through the hills and valleys of the wild and rugged Morvan region. The area is a large National Park, the villages are small and scattered. Finally skirting the lake by the dam of Pannesière-Chaumard, we come to Château-Chinon.

Map references

Saulieu	4°14′E 47°17′N
St Brisson	4°06′E 47°16′N
Saut de Gouloux	4°04′E 47°15′N
Montsauche	4°02′E 47°13′N
Quarré-les-Tombes	4°00′E 47°23′N
Lormes	3°49′E 47°18′N
Vauclaix	3°49′E 47°14′N
Barrage de Pannesière-Chaumard	3°53′E 47°10′N
Château-Chinon	3°56′E 47°04′N

Detour

St Léger Vauban	4°03′E 47°24′N
Abbey of la Pierre-qui-Vire	4°05′E 47°22′N

Route shown pp. 106-7.

Travels in Burgundy

Breakfast at Saulieu.

Ideally the weather will be pleasantly warm for your tour. If so, I recommend you buy some tasty morsels for a picnic from Saulieu before setting out across the Morvan. Although there are villages with good restaurants, amid such natural beauty the advantages of having a picnic are obvious.

The Morvan (La Montagne Noire)

The Morvan, Burgundy's watershed, and away from the main highway, is mostly a rough unfertile area. Its greatest asset is its natural beauty — forests, hills, valleys, rivers, lakes, reservoirs and streams — which make it an ideal terrain for walking (a hiking trail crosses it from Vézelay (N) to Autun (S)), camping, shooting, fishing, canoeing and sailing. It has no real centre but the rugged south is more attractive than the north.

This granite region in the heart of mostly calcareous Burgundy, and now one of the 23 Regional Natural parks of France, has always been considered poor and backward. Apart from carpentry, there were few ways men could earn a living. Many of them emigrated to better land in other parts of France. The women left behind became famous throughout France as wet nurses. In the last century, many a Parisian child spent their early years in the Morvan.

It is still not a prosperous region. But cleared forests and drained marshes have helped to make it more suitable for agriculture and pasturing cattle. Also, tourism, by encouraging the building of hotels and other types of accommodation, and leisure activities, it is attracting visitors looking for a peaceful holiday in natural surroundings.

Take the D977bis from Saulieu skirting the small lakes which are such a feature of the Morvan. Before visiting St Brisson (D20) it is worth going a little further on the D977 to Gouloux and, more especially, to the beautiful waterfall at Saut de Gouloux. A little further still brings you to Montsauche, the highest station in the Morvan.

St Brisson

From the Maison du Parc at St Brisson, the administrative centre for the Morvan Regional Park, you can collect detailed maps and news of any events/festivals coinciding with your visit. There is also an exhibition of the flora of the area. Note the Musée de la Resistance. The area was heavily involved with the Resistance in the Second World War, and driving through the small hamlets you may notice many monuments to the fighters.

North from St Brisson (D6/10) the Fôret au Duc offers attractive walks down to the river Cure. In the forest there is a stone commemorating the first parachute delivery of arms and radios from England.

Lunch at Les Lavauts (D10 en route for Quarré-les-Tombes) unless you are picnicing.

Quarré-les-Tombes

Nearby Quarré-les-Tombes is so named for the sarcophagi (6th- to 9th-century) that surround the 16th-century church. No-one really knows why they are there (and some say these are just the few remaining, once there were over a thousand). Theories are rife — the most common and likely is that a sarcophagus maker worked here, the most fun is that they rained down from heaven to give decent Christian burials to those who died fighting the Saracens.

Detour

East of Quarré-les-Tombes (D55 to St Léger Vauban, birthplace of the Maréchal, then turn right) lies the abbey of Ste Marie de la Pierre-qui-Vire. The monastery, founded 1850, is run by a Bénédictine order which currently has a community of nearly a hundred. Visitors, male or female, are welcome to join their services and there is an exhibition of the monks' working life at the entrance. The monks make and sell cream cheeses. The stone-that-rocks of the title is on the right as you arrive. It is not known whether it is man-made or not, but legend has it that it rocks unaided each Christmas Eve.

West of Quarré-les-Tombes follow the D128 to St Martin-du-Puy and the D944 to Lormes. From Vauclaix the route winds gently down to the dam at Pannesière-Chaumard. Continue directly into Château-Chinon (D944) or cross the dam (D303) and follow the delightful road westwards around the banks of the lake via Chaumard to Corancy. Follow the D37 to Château-Chinon in the south.

Château-Chinon

Château-Chinon, a small town and the Morvan's capital, does not have much character. But its pleasant enough as a holiday resort and its site, astride a ridge, is picturesque. And it makes a very good centre for exploring the Morvan. In times past it has been a Gallic settlement, a Roman camp and a feudal castle. For a good circular panoramic view of the region, climb to La Calvaire, the town's highest point.

François Mitterand was mayor of the town from 1959 to 1981. Since his presidency he has donated the gifts received during his term of office from countries worldwide to a permanent exhibition in Château-Chinon. A museum has been created to house them, the Musée du Septennat, in the 18th-century buildings of the Convent of St Clair. As the gifts are mainly presented by heads of state they offer samples of the best of each country's crafts. It is an unusual and fascinating collection.

Dinner and overnight at Château-Chinon.

Auberge de l'Altre
Les Lavauts
89632 Quarré-les-Tombes
Tel: (86) 32 20 79

A charming hostel set in the country, converted from a farmhouse building and stables. Delicious homemade cookery by M. Salamolard who is a true enthusiast for fresh honest produce. There is a spectacular wine list of 200 vintages and an equally spectacular menu devoted to puddings alone. It comprises separate sections for patisserie, fruit tarts, hot puddings and sorbets and ice creams.

Closed:	January, Tuesday evenings and Wednesdays
Credit cards:	Carte Bleu, Am.Ex, Euro, Diners
Food:	Three star food at two star prices
Rating:	★★

Aux Vieux Morvan
Château-Chinon
Tel: (86) 85 05 01

Good food and accommodation in the centre of this small town. Wonderful views of the surrounding country can be had from here.

Closed:	Sundays (restaurant)
Rooms:	23
Credit cards:	Euro, Visa
Rating	★★

Le Lion d'Or
10 rue Fossés
Château-Chinon
Tel: (86) 85 13 56

Another modest yet good value establishment.

Closed:	Sunday evenings and Mondays
Rooms:	10
Credit cards:	Euro, Visa
Rating:	★★

CHÂTEAU-CHINON: USEFUL INFORMATION

Tourist Office:	Rue Champlain
	Tel: (86) 85 06 58
Population:	2,679
General Interest:	Museum (President's)

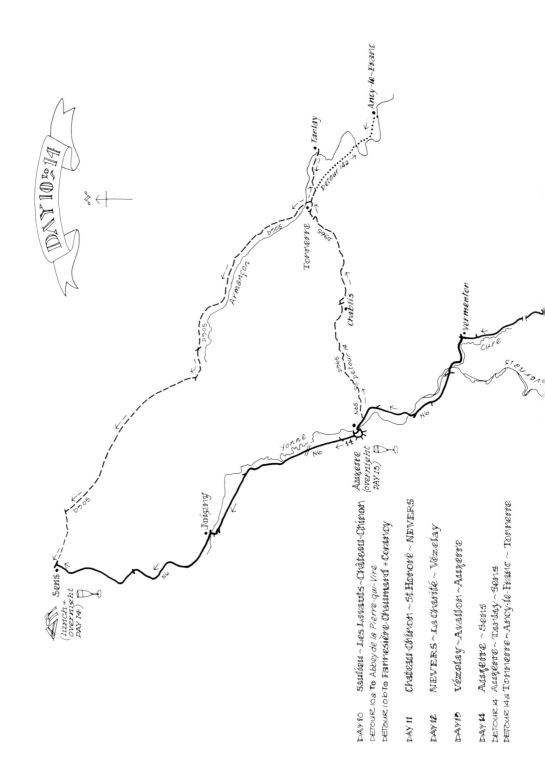

DAY 10 TO 14

Sens
(lunch + overnight
DAY 14)

Joigny

Auxerre
(overnight
DAY 13)

N6

Yonne

N65

Detour 14a

Chablis

D965

Tonnerre

D905

Armançon

D905

D905

Tarnlay

Detour 14a

Ancy-le-Franc

Vermenton

Cure

Sereins

N6

DAY 10   Saulieu ~ Les Lavaults ~ Château-Chinon
DETOUR 10a To Abbey de la Pierre-qui-Vire
DETOUR 10b To Farmesière Chaumard + Corancy

DAY 11   Château-Chinon ~ St-Honoré ~ NEVERS

DAY 12   NEVERS ~ La Charité ~ Vézelay

DAY 13   Vézelay ~ Avallon ~ Auxerre

DAY 14   Auxerre ~ Sens
DETOUR 14 Auxerre ~ Tarnlay ~ Sens
DETOUR 14a Tonnerre ~ Ancy-le-Franc ~ Tonnerre

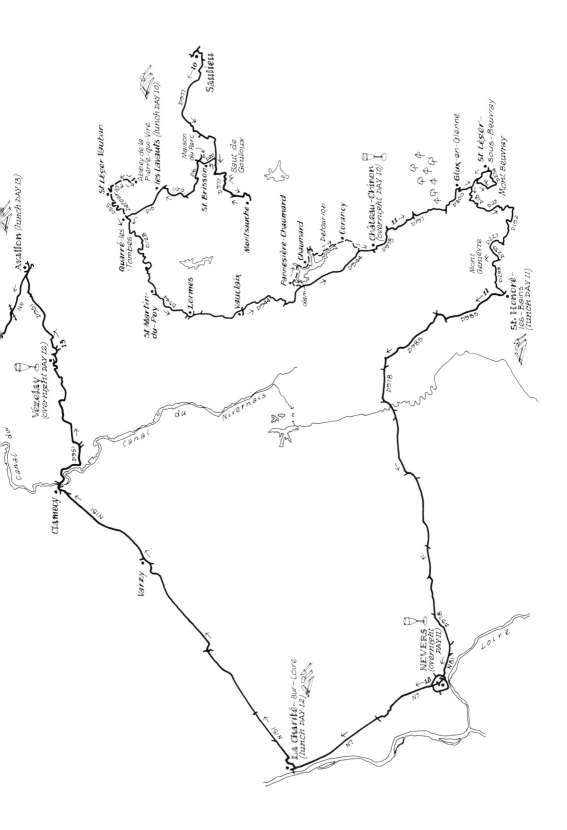

Avallon (lunch DAY 13)

St Léger-Vauban

Abbey de la
Pierre-qui-Vire

les Lavaults (lunch DAY 10)

Quarré-les-
Tombes

Saulieu

Maison
du Parc

St Brisson

Saut de
Gouloux

Montsauche

St Martin-
du-Puy

Lormes

Vauclaix

Pannesière-Chaumard

Chaumard

Détour10b

Corancy

Château-Chinon
(overnight DAY 10)

Gilux-en-Glenne

St Léger-
sous-Beuvray
Mont Beuvray

Vézelay
(overnight DAY 12)

Clamecy

Canal du Nivernais

Mont
Genèvre

St. Honoré-
les-Bains
(lunch DAY 11)

Varzy

Loire

NEVERS
(overnight
DAY 11)

La Charité-sur-Loire
(lunch DAY 12)

DAY 11

Château-Chinon, Mont Beuvray, St Honoré-les-Bains, Nevers: approx. 118 km (74 miles)

First stop today is Mont Beuvray, once it was Bibracte the fortress capital of the Eduens and scene of Vercingétorix' successful career, before his Roman defeat. Lunch is at St Honoré-les-Bains, whose spa has been popular since Roman times. In the afternoon you reach Nevers, capital of the Nivernais.

Overnight at Nevers.

Map references

Château-Chinon	3°56'E 47°04'N
Mont Beuvray	4°03'E 46°55'N
Mont Genièvre	3°54'E 46°55'N
St Honoré-les-Bains	3°51'E 46°54'N
Nevers	3°10'E 47°00'N

Route shown p. 106-7.

St Honoré-les-Bains

Depart Château-Chinon.

Drive along the D978 eastwards and then turn south (D197/300/18) via Glux-en-Glenne to Mont Beuvray. The D274 leads to its summit.

Mont Beuvray

At 821 m, Mont Beuvray is one of the Morvan's highest points. Apart from excavations, which were started by M. Bulliot, an archaeologist from Autun, in the last century, there is not a great deal to see here that would tell you that this was Bibracte, fortress capital of the Eduens. As at Cluny, you will have to use your imagination.

It was here that Vercingétorix was appointed Commander-in-Chief of the Gallic tribes before the disastrous Alésian campaign. After his defeat by the Romans, Bibracte was replaced by Autun as capital. In a peaceful Gaul it was far better placed for trade. You can see the old Roman city from here, also the Signal d'Uchon and Mont-St-Vincent and, on a clear day, even as far as the Jura and the Alps.

Although trees mostly cover the ramparts and town, hopefully much of what lies below will eventually be revealed. There is a landmark indicator to show the importance of the town's position. Some of the articles excavated may be seen in the Musée Rolin at Autun. There is also a small exhibition (scale-model, photographs, etc.) in the Town Hall of nearby Saint-Léger-sous-Beuvray, and where the road to Mont Beuvray starts.

Take the D18/27/192/227/299 to St Honoré-les-Bains, via Mont Genièvre.

St Honoré-les-Bains

St Honoré-les-Bains, spa and popular Morvan tourist centre was a health resort even in Roman times. Its sulphuric, arsenical and radioactive water is still used to cure asthma and bronchitis. Around it lies the Deffond forest; nearby is that stretch of water, the Etang du Seu: Autun can be reached via the gorges of the Canche, a varied and picturesque route.

Lunch at St Honoré-les-Bains.

Follow the D985/978 direct to Nevers.

Nevers

The Nivernais region is predominantly a crossroads. Small hills and plateaux merge with the Morvan Massif in the east and slope towards the Loire valley in the west. From here come the white wines of Pouilly-sur-Loire, Chasselas and Blanc Fumé, noted for their subtle flavour, and red wine from Cosne-sur-Loire.

Its capital is Nevers, on a hill overlooking the Nièvre river and a few kilometres from the confluence of the Loire and Allier. From its Grand Pont one has a good view of the old town — gables, steep roofs, towers and spires, spread out below its sturdy cathedral and elegant ducal palace. Another old Roman city, it was once known as Noviodunum Aeduorum. Situated on important trade routes between Switzerland, Flanders and the coast, also on the pilgrims' way between Vézelay and Compostella, it became a trade, religious and artistic centre.

Nevers was long famous for its faïence and glassware. When Louis de Gonzague became Duke of Nivernais in 1565, he brought with him from Italy a number of artists and artisans. He set up a faïence industry between 1575 and 1585. The Conrade brothers, also from Italy, and masters of their craft, taught their skills to the local artisans, who eventually evolved their own particular styles. The pottery industry reached its zenith in the mid-17th century, but was dealt a grave blow by the Revolution. There is a good collection of Nevers faïence to be seen in the Municipal museum.

Take time to wander round the old streets, visit the 14th-century Croux gate, the half-Romanesque, half-Gothic St Cyr and Ste Julitte cathedral, St Etienne church (completed in 1097), the ducal palace (11th- to 16th-century, and Renaissance), now the law courts.

Nevers has some fairly recent religious connections. In the chapel of Convent St Gildard lies the body of Bernadette Soubiros, St Bernadette of Lourdes, who entered the convent in 1866 and died here in 1879.

Dinner and overnight at Nevers.

Hôtel Henry Robert

47 Avenue du Général d'Espeuilles
58360 Saint-Honoré-les-Bains
Tel: (86) 30 72 33

Lunch in sumptuous style in this splendid hotel set in its own gardens. The decorative brickwork on the facade and the elegant furnishings inside give this establishment the air of a private house smoothly run by the owner Madame Martine Poulet.

Closed:	30 September to 1 May
Rooms:	14
Credit cards:	Visa, Mastercard, Am.Ex.
Food:	Filet de boeuf aux girolles, Saumon de Loire, Saupiquet de Morvan
Rating:	★★★

ST HONORÉ-LES-BAINS: USEFUL INFORMATION

Tourist Office:	Place F. Bazot
	Tel: (86) 30 71 70
Population:	831
Facilities:	Casino, Spa

Hôtel de Morvan
28 Rue de Mouesse
58000 Nevers
Tel: (86) 61 14 16

A small hotel with modest room prices and equally modest menus. Specialities of the house are Parfait aux foies de volailles and Escalope de sandre aux petits légumes.

Closed:	2-20 January, 2-20 July, Monday evenings and Wednesdays
Rooms:	8
Facilities:	Restaurant
Credit cards:	Carte Bleu
Rating:	★★

Auberge Ste Marie
25 Rue de Mouesse
58000 Nevers
Tel: (86) 61 10 02

Closed:	February and Mondays
Rooms:	17
Facilities:	Parking, terrace
Credit cards:	Carte Bleu, Visa, Mastercard
Food:	Specialities include: Trout Ste Marie in a pastry case, and a wide choice of desserts
Rating:	★★★

NEVERS: USEFUL INFORMATION

Tourist Office:	31 Rue des Ramparts Tel: (86) 59 07 03
Population:	44,777
Facilities:	Golf course (4 km)
General Interest:	Cathedral, museums, old buildings

Vézelay

DAY 12

Nevers, La Charité-sur-Loire, Clamecy, Vézelay: approx. 100 km (63 miles)

La Charité-sur-Loire has a long history of caring for travellers. After lunching here we continue northeast crossing the top of the Morvan to Clamecy, set in beautiful countryside before ending the afternoon at Vézelay, for so long a place of pilgrimage.

Overnight at Vézelay.

Map references
Nevers   3°10′E 47°00′N
La Charité-sur-Loire   3°02′E 47°11′N
Clamecy   3°32′E 47°27′N
Vézelay   3°44′E 47°28′N

Route shown p. 106-7.

Breakfast at Nevers.

Depart Nevers northwards on the N7 to La Charité-sur-Loire.

La Charité-sur-Loire

La Charité-sur-Loire is dominated by the towers of Notre Dame, or St Croix, another Romanesque jewel and place of pilgrimage. The town stands on a hill on the Burgundian side of the Loire, which is crossed by a quaint 16th-century bridge, a reminder of the time when the Loire was an important navigable river and the town a great port.

Charité was first known as 'Seyr', 'of the sun', a Phoenician word. Its inhabitants were converted to Christianity and a monastery and church were founded here at about the beginning of the 8th century. Although this brought prosperity at first, later Arab invasions devastated the town. The Bénédictine priory and church, dependencies of Cluny and the largest in France after Cluny, were built in the second half of the 11th century. This and the town's prosperity attracted crowds of travellers, pilgrims and especially beggars. The good fathers were famous for their charity. 'Go to charity' became a saying of the time for those needing help, hence the town's name.

Unfortunately, during medieval times, Charité's importance as a bridgehead across the Loire brought its possession into dispute between the Burgundians and the Kings of France. In 1429, Charles VII told Jeanne d'Arc to retake the town, then changed his mind, leaving her to her fate. In 1559, a fire lasting 3 days destroyed the monastery, part of the church and 200 houses. The Wars of Religion prevented the reconstruction of the monastery and church, and it was not until the 17th century, under the direction of Nicholas Colbert, that it was partly restored to its old glory. However, the priests came to accept its dilapidated condition and by the time of the Revolution, there were only about a dozen monks inhabiting the monastery. In the last century, Prosper Merimée, novelist and Minister of Fine Arts, saved the church from destruction. Much restoration has been carried out since then.

The best view of it is from the square of the Bénédictines. Another one, and of the old town too, is from Rue du Clos, by the Esplanade.

Lunch at La Charité-sur-Loire.

Follow the N151 to Clamecy.

Clamecy

'Town of beautiful reflections and supple hills', wrote novelist Romain Rolland of his native town. Perched on a spur overlooking rivers Beuvron and Yonne and the canal de Nivernais, this old town is set in the heart of a pretty countryside in the Morvan's northwest corner. Its old town of crooked narrow streets is delightful just to wander round. Visit its church, St Martin (13th-, 14th- and 15th-century). Flamboyant style and richly decorated — episodes from the life of St Martin may be seen carved on its portal. On leaving the church, take Rue de la Tour, Rue Temple and Grenier à Sel (Rue G. Merle). On descending La Rue Bourgeoise note L'Hôtel Moor de Tannère, now the cultural centre Romain Rolland. There is also a museum to him and his work. His birthplace is next to 16th-century (restored) Hôtel de Bellegarde (built by the Duke of Bellegarde when exiled here by the king). Visit the Bethléem quarter with its aged chapel which belonged to the Bishops of Bethléem; large flower-filled Parc Vauvert and the quarter of the timber trade.

Because of its good position on the river, Clamecy became the centre of the Morvan's timber trade. In the 16th century, Jean Rouvet, a Paris merchant, started a business which floated logs from the Morvan to Paris. However, the opening of the Nivernais canal in 1834 and later the railway put paid to this enterprise. A legacy perhaps of this long-running business is that Clamecy now has one of the largest wood-processing plants in France. The town has honoured Jean Rouvet with a bust above the Pont de Bethléem. As no one knew what he looked like so many centuries after his death, the sculptor sent them an old bust of Napoleon he'd once made, hoping that no one would know the difference. Luckily for him he was not found out until after he'd been paid.

Take the D951 to Vézelay.

Vézelay

Vézelay's famous basilica Ste Madeleine is situated on a hilltop, a serene sentinel of the Morvan's wild countryside. My first view of the town was of the basilica's steeple thrusting high above the surrounding climbing rooftops. The walk to the church via Promenade des Fosses (leave your car in Champ de Foire) or by Grande Rue is the steep way trodden by many weary pilgrims over the centuries.

Pilgrims would gather in the large nathex before entering the church proper. Above its entrance is a magnificent tympanum, where sits an enormous Christ (notice the particularly large hands) with his twelve apostles either side. They are receiving the Holy Spirit in the form of rays from his hands. The tympanum represents the Mission of the Apostles after the Resurrection.

The church beyond appears rather plain, perhaps eastern-looking. Particularly to note are the realistic capitals (about 100) on the nave pillars, possibly the work of five different unknown artists. One especially meriting attention is the Moulin Mystique (mystic mill) — a man passes grain into a mill while another collects the flour in his hands — which is supposed to represent Christ grinding the corn of Mosaic law into the nourishing flour of the gospels.

On a grassy slope behind the basilica, a cross marks the spot where St Bernard preached the Second Crusade in 1146. Some 100,000 horsemen are supposed to have answered his summons. Among them were Louis VII of France with his then wife, Eleanor of Aquitaine. Richard the Lionheart and Philippe-August of France met at Vézelay before embarking on the Third Crusade.

Ste Madeleine was founded in the 9th century and its abbey came under the influence of Cluny in the 11th. After it was burned down in 1120, the rebuilt church, completed in 1215, harboured the supposed remains of Ste Marie Madeleine, the beloved sinner, which made it an important place of pilgrimage. Roads to Jerusalem and Compostella crossed here. However, in 1279, after Pope Boniface VIII had declared that her mortal remains were held by St Maximin in Provence, pilgrimages fell off. Secular canons replaced the monks; it was badly pillaged by the Huguenots in 1569, and it was partly burned down during the Revolution. Its monastic buildings were later sold as national property and destroyed. Only the church was left standing. Restoration began in the middle of the 19th century by Viollet-le-Duc.

Vézelay is still an influential religious centre in France. The surrounding well-preserved medieval village — churches, ramparts, gates, 15th-, 16th- and 17th-century houses — is well worth exploring.

Dinner and overnight at Vézelay.

A la Bonne Foi
91 Rue Camille Barrère
58400 La Charité-sur-Loire
Tel: (86) 70 15 77

A modest chef/proprietor run restaurant with 3 fixed price menus and an à la carte. Specialities of the house are fish, foie gras and an imposing dessert trolley.

Closed:	Sunday evenings and Mondays
Credit cards:	Visa, Euro, Diners
Rating:	★★

Hôtel le Grand Monarque
33 Quai Clemenceau
58400 La Charité-sur-Loire
Tel: (86) 70 21 73

In the restaurant of this small hotel, which is a member of Relais Gastronomique, all cooking is done with fresh produce in season. The extensive à la carte menu changes daily, specialities of which include Petite salade de fruits de mer, Turbot aux petits légumes, Filet of beef with mushrooms.

Closed:	Last 2 weeks in February and Wednesdays from November to March
Credit cards:	Am.Ex, Visa, Euro, Diners
Rating:	★★★

LA CHARITÉ-SUR-LOIRE: USEFUL INFORMATION

Tourist Office:	49 Grande Rue
	Tel: (86) 70 16 12
Population:	6,422

119

Hôtel le Pontet
Vézelay
Tel: (86) 33 24 40

Although this hotel has no restaurant it has lovely views and a quiet, secluded garden.

Closed:	15 November to 1 April
Rooms:	8
Credit cards:	Am.Ex., Euro, Visa
Rating:	★★

La Poste et Lion d'Or
Place Champ-de-Foire
Vézelay
Tel: (86) 33 27 57

Closed:	End November to 15 March
Rooms:	46
Facilities:	Restaurant, Garden, Parking
Credit cards:	Am.Ex., Diners, Visa
Rating:	★★

Restaurant Bougainville
26 Rue St Etienne
89450 Vézelay
Tel: (86) 33 27 57

A very reasonable restaurant specialising in regional dishes.

Closed:	30 November to 1 February and Tuesdays
Credit cards:	Visa, Carte Bleu, Mastercard
Rating:	★★

VÉZELAY: USEFUL INFORMATION

Tourist Office:	Rue St Pierre Tel: (86) 33 23 69
Population:	582
General Interest:	Splendid views from tower of Basilica Ste Madeleine

DAY 13

Vézelay, Avallon, Auxerre: approx. 65 km (40 miles)

A short drive to Avallon in the morning allows plenty of time to explore the ancient fortifications and to walk around the old town before lunch. The afternoon is spent at Auxerre on the river Yonne.

Overnight at Auxerre.

Map references

Vézelay	3°44′E 47°28′N
Avallon	3°55′E 47°29′N
Auxerre	3°34′E 47°47′N

Route shown p. 106-7.

Breakfast at Vézelay.

Leaving Vézelay, take a short drive (D957) to Avallon.

Avallon

Avallon takes its name from the Gallic word Aballo, which by the 10th century had become Avallonem Castrum. Most strategically sited on a granite rock, between two ravines and overlooking several valleys, it was the key to medieval Burgundy. Often attacked, it has passed through many hands. It has been burned down, pillaged and its inhabitants slaughtered. Eventually, when no longer of any military importance, the French king, Louis XIV, sold the ramparts to the municipality, who turned them into a promenade walk surrounding the town.

To explore the old town's fortifications, leave your car in the car park opposite St Lazare, whose old church dates back a long way, certainly before the 9th century, of which only the crypt remains. About the year 1000, a bone from the skull of St Lazarus was presented to the church by a Duke of Burgundy. Hence its name. As this relic was supposed to ward off leprosy, pilgrims flocked here in such large numbers that the church had to be enlarged. Today's main attraction is its portals.

Continue to the little gateway, Petite Porte, once strongly fortified and used by foot-travellers; then its bastion, and eventually to the Tower of Eschanguet (the Elected), also known as the Cowherd's Tower. It lodged the town's cowherd hence the name of the next street, Rue de la Vachère. Turn left, take Rue Masquée on the right. Keeping left, follow Rue du College into Rue Fort Mahon. You will notice the Gally Spur, flanked by a watch tower, 1591. Steps lead down to a terrace. The Chapter Tower, appearing on your left, built 1450-54, is still in good condition. Next comes the Promenade de la Petite Porte, planted with lime trees, where you can admire the view. The Gaujard Tower, built 1438, restored 1870, opens on to a terrace and you are back at Petite Porte where you started the tour. If you continue on into the town, you will be in the original Roman part, and the castle, which had so many different owners, depending on who was then occupying the town. A salt store, Law Courts, museum (mineralogy, prehistory, regional archaeology, paintings, etc.), clock tower (used for keeping watch from 1467 onwards), the Provost's House (17th-century) and the town house of the Prince of Condé (16th- to 17th-century) are in the vicinity.

Lunch at Avallon.

Follow the N6 to Auxerre.

Auxerre

Auxerre (Roman Autissiodurum), capital of Lower Burgundy, overlooking the Yonne river, is another town whose medieval walls have been replaced by boulevards. As a northern gateway to the province, it makes an excellent starting place should you plan a holiday on Burgundy's rivers and canals on your next visit. The best view of the town is from the east bank of the Yonne. The old towers and spires of its three main churches are silhouetted gracefully above the quayside trees.

Its most noteworthy church is St Etienne (13th- to 16th-century; crypt 11th), reckoned to be one of the finest cathedrals in France. Note especially the stained-glass windows of the ambulatory, the Romanesque crypt and the treasure-room.

St Etienne has some important historical connections. English and Burgundian leaders met here in 1422 to plan their operations against France: in the square outside, Napoleon met Marshal Ney after Napoleon's famous escape from Elba. A disguised Joan of Arc came through Auxerre on her way to meet the Dauphin at Chinon, and returned through it after defeating the English at Orléans, triumphantly leading the Dauphin to his coronation at Reims.

Dinner and overnight at Auxerre.

Les Capuchins
6 Avenue P. Doumer
89200 Avallon
Tel: (86) 34 06 52

This small hotel and restaurant is more like a delightful country house though set in the centre of Avallon. Daniel Aublanc is the creative and committed chef and Mme Aublanc your cheerful hostess. They buy fresh produce daily from the market.

Closed:	10-20 October, 20 December-20 January, Tuesday evenings and Wednesdays
Credit cards:	Carte Bleu, Visa, Mastercard
Food:	Pork fillet with cream and thyme, Fillet of beef with paprika, 'le poisson du marché'
Rating:	★★★

AVALLON: USEFUL INFORMATION

Tourist Office:	6 rue Bocquillot Tel: (86) 34 14 19
Population:	9,186
General Interest:	Ancient buildings, walled town, museum

Hôtel de Seignelay
2 Rue de Pont
89000 Auxerre
Tel: (86) 52 03 48

This is a timber-framed old coaching inn with very reasonable room prices. It has a nice open courtyard set with tables under shady trees where meals may be served.

Closed:	10 January-10 February, Mondays between November and June

Rooms: 23
Facilities: Garage
Credit cards: Carte Bleu, Visa, Mastercard,
                  Access
Food: Jambon Chablisienne, Coq au
                  vin, and snails
Rating: ★★

If you fancy a more adventurous meal try the following restaurant, one of the gastronomic highlights of the town.

Le Jardin Gourmand
56 Boulevard Vauban
89000 Auxerre
Tel: (86) 51 53 52

Sit in the pretty dining room or eat al fresco on the terrace. The chef, Pierre Boussereau, is truly inventive, cooking such varied dishes as wild asparagus flan, lobster with basil, rabbit with honey and plaice with rosemary, all to be found on the set menu. His wife, Sylvie, looks after the cellar with an extensive selection of Chablis.

Closed: 1 August-21 November,
                  February, Sunday evenings
                  (except July) and Mondays
Credit cards: Carte Bleu, Visa
Rating: ★★

AUXERRE: USEFUL INFORMATION

Tourist Office: 1-2, Quai République
                      Tel: (86) 52 06 19
Population: 40,698
General Interest: Cathedral and Abbey

DAY 14

Auxerre, Sens: approx. 62 km (39 miles)

Leave Auxerre and head north to Sens, famous for its cathedral, for your last day. Depending on your schedule you are now fairly close to Paris and can begin your homeward journey after lunch. Alternatively, if you have the time, a detour outlines a trip through the Chablis region close to Auxerre, and visits to a couple of châteaux before heading north to Sens — where you could spend the night.

Map references
Auxerre   3°34'E 47°47'N
Sens   3°17'E 48°13'N

Detour 1
Chablis   3°47'E 47°48'N
Tonnerre   3°58'E 47°52'N
Tanlay   4°06'E 47°51'N

Detour 2
Ancy-le-Franc   4°10'E 47°47'N

Route shown pp. 106-7.

Sens Cathedral

Travels in Burgundy

Breakfast at Auxerre.

Leave Auxerre and drive direct to Sens (N6).

Sens

Sens, another northern gateway to Burgundy, is either the first or last place people will see depending on which way they are travelling. Like Auxerre, its ramparts have been replaced by boulevards, but its cathedral is more famous and considered more beautiful. Once the seat of an important Bishopric and one of France's most powerful cities, it has declined since the Revolution.

Sens takes its name from Senones, one of the most powerful of the Gallic tribes. They even managed to capture Rome in the year 390. At the time of the Roman occupation, it was one of the capitals of Gaul. During medieval times, the increasing strength of the Bishopric can be measured by the motto of the cathedral, CAMPONT, which stands for Chartres, Auxerre, Meaux, Paris, Orléans, Nevers and Troyes, over which cities Sens once presided.

The cathedral of St Etienne, started about 1140, was the first of the great Gothic cathedrals to be built in France. Its proportions are faultless, a serene harmony of mass and line with no striving after effects. St Etienne himself stands on a pillar of the central doorway. Inside note the beautiful stained-glass windows (12th- to 17th-century), magnificently-carved pillars and a rich display of treasures. It contains one of the best collections of vestments and religious objects in France.

The architecture was copied in other church buildings. After a fire in 1174, which almost destroyed Canterbury cathedral, a French architect, William of Sens was chosen to help in its reconstruction, which took only five years. Although old parts saved from the fire were preserved, there are now many similarities between the two cathedrals. Thomas à Becket stayed at Sens, and in the nearby abbey of Columba, after falling into disgrace with English king, Henry II. He lived in one of the houses of the Canon's cloister near the northern tower of the cathedral. The people here were greatly shocked by his subsequent murder, which resulted in his cult as a martyr. His story is represented in some of the stained glass windows, of which only four remain. They show Henry II and Becket trying to be reconciled, Becket's return to England, his welcome and preaching, and then his murder by the four knights.

Detour 1

Take the D965 to Chablis.

Chablis wine region

The Chablis country, lying between Auxerre and the valley Armançon, the most northerly of Burgundy's wine producing regions, is not very large. Hundreds of small vineyards contribute their grapes to the Chablis wine presses. Fine dry (white) wines of a beautiful golden colour are produced in this wine region. The most famous, Chablis's Grand Crus — Les Vaudesir, Les Clos, Grenouille, Les Preuses, Valmun, Blanchot and Bougros — are grown on the steep slopes of the right bank of the Serein river.

Chablis

Chablis, a small pleasant town beside the Serein, could be called another Burgundian gateway, the Porte d'Or, the golden gate which leads into the first stage of the wine road. A promenade borders the Serein. Its main treasure is its church of St Martin, a small version of the cathedral at Sens. The first church here sheltered the relics of St Martin during 9th-century Norman raids. This one dates from the 12th century. An oddity here are the horse shoes nailed to a Romanesque door. Perhaps they were put there by travellers who felt in need of a blessing before setting out on their journey.

Tonnerre

Continue D965 to Tonnerre, another very old and delightful market town situated beside the Armançon, surrounded by vineyards and greenery. Above it on a rock stands 16th-century St-Pierre offering good views from its terrace of the undulating countryside. Below, at the foot of the cliff on the north side is the Fosse Dionne (divine ditch), a blueish-green pool, which in ancient times was the town's only source of water. More recently it has been used as a public wash-place.

Tonnerre's most interesting building is its old hospital, founded in 1293 by Marguerite of Burgundy, the interior is similar in many respects to that of Hôtel Dieu in Beaune, built about 150 years later. In 1630, it acted temporarily as the parish church while Notre-Dame in picturesque Rue Michel, was being rebuilt. Note the tombstones set in the floor from that period. Of particular interest is the beautiful sepulchre of the Marquis de Louvois, Count of Tonnerre and Minister of Louis XIV, by Giradon and Desjardins; and the statue of the foundress herself in white marble, work of Bridan; also the Sepulchre au Vieil Hôpital in a small chapel, which represents the death of Christ (look especially at the faces of the disciples, particularly the Virgin Mary). This last-named was presented by a rich burgher in 1454.

Continue east to Tanlay, D965.

Tanlay

Here you will find one of France's most magnificent and celebrated châteaux. Its approach is through a large wooded park and down a long double avenue of elms. First comes elegant Petit Château, the Cours Verte (noted for well-tended grass) and a bridge over a wide moat to Cour d'Honneur and Grand Château.

Tanlay's oldest part was erected in the 16th century over the remains of an old castle by Louis de Montmorency, mother of the Coligny brothers, Protestant leaders in the Wars of Religion, and subsequently added to by Andelot de Coligny, one of her sons. It was bought and further embellished and added to by Porticelli d'Hemery, who used the celebrated architect, Le Muet, who had a passion for symmetry, and has been termed a precursor of the Louis XIV style. He added a magnificent stretch of water to the garden, 530 metres long and 25 metres wide, which was named the Grand Canal.

In the Wars of Religion Tanlay was on the Protestant side. You will notice in the Tower room that the theme of the paintings reflects the rivalry between the Catholics and Protestants at Catherine de Médici's court. The apartments are sumptuously decorated, especially the Long Gallery, the vestibule, the Grand Salon, the Dining Room and staircase.

From Tanlay take the D965/905 to Sens.

Detour 2

If time you could go further south via D905 to Ancy-le-Franc.

This is another of France's beautiful Renaissance châteaux. Its exterior, austere and formal, resembling a minor palace, lacks the ornamentation of Tanlay. But its interior is even more magnificent. There are 19 galleries and apartments to visit, exquisitely decorated by Niccolo dell Abbate and pupils of Primatice. To note especially here is the Salle des Gardes (splendid fireplace and chimney-piece), the chapel, the Hall of Roman Emperors and the blue and gold Chambre du Roi.

16th-century Ancy-le-Franc was designed by Serlio, an Italian employed at the court of François I. Many kings have stayed here, also such notables as Vauban and Madame de Sévigné (she wrote many of her famous letters in a room on the first floor).

Return to Tonnerre and continue to Sens (D905).

Dinner and overnight at Sens.

Hostellerie du Clos
Rue Jules Rathier
89800 Chablis
Tel: (86) 42 10 63

The setting for Michel Vignaud's restaurant is an historic building converted from a set of old almshouses surrounding a courtyard, which includes a 12th-century chapel. These delightful ancient surroundings are contrasted inside with stylish modern decor and up-to-the-minute cuisine. You can lunch modestly on the set price menu or you can treat yourself to the Menu Gourmand at three times as much.

Closed:	January, Wednesdays and Thursday lunchtimes between October and May
Rooms:	26
Credit cards:	Am.Ex, Visa, Diners, Mastercard
Food:	Terrine de Sandre soufflée au Chablis and Homard Breton aux champignons sauvages
Rating:	★★★/★★★★★

Hôtel de Paris et de la Poste
97 Rue de la République
89100 Sens
Tel: (86) 65 17 43

This is the grand old coaching house hotel of the town, with an air of ancient comfort. The menu includes 2 and 3 course set menus and there is also a Menu Dégustation where the chef will serve you small portions of several dishes of the day.

Closed:	Open all year
Rooms:	26 + suites
Facilities:	Garage, bar, restaurant
Credit cards:	Carte Bleu, Am.Ex, Diners, Access
Rating:	★★★★

SENS: USEFUL INFORMATION

Tourist Office:	Place J. Jaurés
	Tel: (86) 65 19 49
Population:	26,961
General Interest:	Cathedral

Recipes
from the Region

MENU 1 ✤❀✤

Gougères

. . .

Meurette de carpe

. . .

Sorbet au marc de Bourgogne

Wine suggestion

A red Burgundy such as a Mercurey or
St-Aubin, or a Beaujolais cru.

Auxerre, Tour de l'Horloge

Gougères

8 fl oz/250 ml water
pinch of salt
3½ oz/100 g butter
5 oz/125 g flour
4-5 eggs
5 oz/125 g gruyère,
diced

Serves 4

Gougères are served warm and should be crisp on the outside and soft inside.

Bring the water, salt and butter to the boil, then remove the pan from the heat and tip in all the flour. Beat vigorously with a wooden spoon until the mixture is smooth and comes away from the sides of the pan and forms a ball. Return the pan to gentle heat and cook for about two minutes, stirring all the time.

Remove the pan from the heat again and beat in the eggs, one at a time. The mixture should be shiny and just fall from the spoon. Don't let it become too runny, if necessary use only part of the last egg. Now stir in the diced cheese.

Butter two baking sheets, and using a spoon, put little mounds of dough onto the baking sheets, keeping them well apart because the gougères spread and rise while baking.

If you wish, brush the gougères with egg beaten with a tablespoon of water in order to glaze them, then put them in a preheated oven 375°F, 190°C, gas 5 and bake for about 45 minutes. They should be crisp and golden brown.

Meurette de carpe

1 carp of 2½-3 lb/1.25-
1.5 kg
1 onion, chopped
3 cloves garlic, chopped
bouquet garni
salt and pepper
1 bottle red burgundy
2 oz/50 g butter
1 oz/25 g flour

for the garnish
1 oz/25 g butter
4 oz/120 g streaky
bacon, cut in thin strips
20 small white onions
salt and pepper
8 triangles of bread
oil for frying
2 tbs chopped parsley

Serves 4

Clean the carp and cut it in pieces. Make a bed of onion and garlic in an ovenproof dish, put the carp on top, tuck in the bouquet garni, season with salt and pepper and pour over the wine. Cover and leave to marinate for 2-3 hours in the refrigerator.

While the fish is marinating, prepare the garnish. Melt a little of the butter and fry the bacon until it is lightly browned. Drain and set aside. Put the onions in a pan with the rest of the butter, 2 tablespoons of water and salt and pepper. Cover and cook gently for 10 minutes until the onions are tender, but don't let them brown. Set them aside.

Preheat the oven to 350°F, 180°C, gas 4 and bake the fish in its marinade in a covered dish for about 20 minutes, or until it flakes easily. Transfer it to a serving dish, discard the head, and keep warm. Strain the liquid into a pan and boil until it has reduced by a third. Blend the flour and butter together to make beurre manié and whisk it into the sauce, a little at a time, until it thickens enough to coat the back of a spoon. Add the bacon and onions, taste for seasoning, pour the sauce over the fish and keep warm for 5 minutes to allow the flavours to blend.

Heat some oil in a frying pan and fry the triangles of bread until golden on both sides. Drain them and arrange them around the edge of the dish.

Sprinkle over the parsley and serve.

Sorbet au marc de Bourgogne
Brandy sorbet

12 oz/370 g sugar
1¼ pt/750 ml water
peel and juice of 1
lemon
¼ pt/150 ml marc or
brandy
2 egg whites

Serves 4

Boil the sugar and water with the lemon peel for 5 minutes, strain it and leave to cool. Add the lemon juice and freeze in a shallow tray or plastic box. After an hour or so, when the mixture starts to set, stir it thoroughly with a fork. Return to the freezer and leave for a further 2 hours. Remove from the freezer and beat in the marc. Beat the egg whites until stiff in a large bowl, add the ice gradually and continue beating. The mixture should become a mass of white foam. Put it into a larger container and return to the freezer until it is set firmly. Serve straight from the freezer, with a little more marc poured over if you wish.

MENU 2 ✢❦

Jambon persillé

.   .   .

Poulet à la vigneronne

.   .   .

Cerises à l'eau-de-vie

Wine suggestion

A white Burgundy — a great one such as a
Meursault or Montrachet for a celebration, or
a Rully or Montagny.

Jambon persillé
Aspic of ham and parsley

6 lb/3 kg uncooked ham
or gammon
2 lb/1 kg veal bones
2 pig's trotters, split
2 onions, studded with
cloves
2 carrots
3 stalks celery
3 sprigs thyme
2 bay leaves
2 tsp black peppercorns
1 bottle dry white
burgundy
2 egg whites
8 tbs chopped parsley
4 shallots, finely
chopped
pepper and salt

Serves 12

If the ham is very salty soak it first in cold water for several hours. Put it in a large pan with the veal bones and trotters, cover with cold water and bring to the boil, then simmer for five minutes. Drain and rinse.

Put the meat, trotters, and bones back in the cleaned pan with the vegetables, herbs, peppercorns and the wine. Add enough cold water to cover the contents by 1 inch/2 cm and bring to the boil. Skim thoroughly, lower the heat and simmer gently for four to five hours or until the ham is easily pierced with a fork.

Remove the pan from the heat and leave to cool for an hour. Then discard the trotters and bones. Lift out the ham, remove the skin and bone and shred the meat with your fingers or with two forks. Discard any gristle.

Reduce the stock by half over high heat, skimming off any fat. Strain the stock through a muslin cloth and taste for seasoning — it should be highly flavoured.

Beat the egg whites lightly, add to the stock and bring to the boil, stirring constantly. Simmer for 25 minutes then strain through a damp cloth and leave to cool. The stock should be clear.

Put the ham, parsley and shallots into a porcelain bowl and ladle over the stock so that it runs down between the meat. There should be just enough stock to cover the meat. Cover with a plate, put a weight on top and chill for at least 12 hours. Serve the ham from the bowl, cut into wedges.

Poulet à la vigneronne
Chicken with grapes

6 chicken pieces
½ pt/300 ml white
burgundy
1 tbs brandy
1 onion, sliced
1 clove garlic, crushed
1 sprig of thyme
1 bay leaf
a few peppercorns
2 oz /50 g butter
salt and pepper
8 oz/250 g green grapes
8 oz/250 g black grapes
¼ pt/150 ml double
cream

Serves 6

Put the wine, brandy, onion, garlic, herbs and peppercorns into a pan, bring slowly to the boil and then leave to cool. When cold pour this marinade over the chicken and leave in the refrigerator for 4-5 hours, or longer if you wish.

Remove the chicken pieces from the marinade, drain and dry with paper towels. Heat the butter in a sauté pan and sauté the chicken on all sides until it is golden brown. Strain the marinade, pour it over the chicken, sprinkle with salt, cover and simmer gently for 20 minutes, or until the chicken is tender. Remove the chicken and keep it warm. Bring the cooking liquid to the boil and reduce a little. Add the grapes and simmer for a further 5 minutes so they are lightly cooked. Finally stir in the cream, bring to the boil, pour over the chicken and serve.

Cerises à l'eau-de-vie
Cherries in brandy

1 lb/500 g ripe firm
cherries with their stalks
4 oz/125 g sugar
1 bottle brandy or clear
preserving spirit

Wash the cherries and put them into a preserving jar. Dissolve the sugar in the brandy and pour over the cherries, making sure they are completely covered. Close tightly and keep in a cool place for at least two months before using.

To serve, put a tot of the brandy and two or three cherries in a small glass or use as a sauce for vanilla ice cream.

MENU 3 ✤❀✤

Escargots à la bourguignonne

. . .

Lapin à la moutarde

. . .

Poires à la beaujolaise

Wine suggestion

An Aligoté if you want to drink a white wine,
or a Mâcon Rouge or Beaujolais-Villages.

Escargots à la bourguignonne
Burgundy Snails

36 snails with shells
2 cloves garlic
2 shallots, chopped finely
2 tbs finely chopped parsley
salt and freshly ground black pepper
6 oz/150 g unsalted butter

Serves 6

It is easy to buy canned snails with their shells in a separate plastic container and the butter takes only a few minutes to prepare.

Crush the garlic with a little salt. Mix it with the shallots and parsley then blend this mixture into the softened butter. Season with salt and pepper. Put ½ teaspoon of butter into each shell and then a snail, which will push the butter to the bottom of the shell. Add more butter to seal the shell. Put the snails in an ovenproof dish, sprinkle a few drops of water on each shell and bake in a preheated oven, 425°F, 220°C, gas 7 for ten minutes. Serve with French bread.

Lapin à la moutarde
Rabbit with mustard sauce

2 rabbits, cut into pieces
3 oz/ 75 g butter
1 tbs oil
thyme
bay leaf
salt and pepper
4 shallots, chopped finely
8 oz/250 g mushrooms, sliced thinly
¼ pt/150 ml white burgundy
2 tbs Dijon mustard
juice of ½ lemon
8 tbs double cream
chopped parsley

Serves 6

Heat 1 oz/25 g butter and the oil and sauté the rabbit until well browned. Season with crushed thyme and bay leaf, and salt and pepper. Cover tightly and cook in a preheated low oven, 325°F, 160°C, gas 3 for 50 minutes. Heat the remaining butter, brown the shallots, add the mushrooms and sauté them. Moisten with the wine and reduce by half. Stir in the mustard, lemon juice and cream and heat through. Put the rabbit pieces in a warm serving dish, pour over the sauce, sprinkle with parsley and serve.

Poires à la beaujolaise

Pears in beaujolais

6 large pears
lemon juice
¾ pt/450 ml beaujolais
6 oz/150 g sugar
a small piece of
cinnamon
1 clove
6 black peppercorns
2 strips orange peel
2 strips lemon peel

Serves 6

Choose ripe but firm pears and peel them, leaving the stalks on. Put them in water acidulated with lemon juice so they don't discolour.

Boil together all the remaining ingredients for 5 minutes, then reduce to a simmer, put in the pears and cook until they are tender — this may take anything from 20 to 45 minutes, depending on the pears.

When they are cooked, lift them carefully from the pan and put them in a dish in which they just fit standing upright. Boil down the syrup till it thickens and has a rich deep colour. Strain it and spoon a little over each pear. Serve cold.

MENU 4 ✤

Salade au lard et au jambon

· · ·

Boeuf à la bourguignonne

· · ·

Gâteau de marrons

Wine suggestion

A young red Burgundy from the Côte d'Or
such as a Beaune or an Aloxe-Corton.

Salade au lard et au jambon
Salad with bacon and ham

salad greens
2 tbs oil
4 oz/120 g streaky
bacon, cut in thin strips
4 tbs wine vinegar
2 oz/ 50 g raw smoked
ham, cut in thin strips
2 tbs finely chopped
mixed fresh herbs

Serves 6

For this salad a mixture of robust leaves such as
cos lettuce, curly endive, escarole, dandelion or
watercress is best.

Wash and dry the salad greens and arrange them
in a large bowl. Heat the oil in a frying pan and
fry the bacon until browned. Keep about 6
tablespoons of the fat in the pan and discard any
excess. Pour the fat and bacon over the greens
and toss well. Add the vinegar to the hot pan,
heat through and pour over the greens. Toss
again, scatter the ham and herbs on top and
serve.

Boeuf à la bourguignonne
Beef with burgundy

3 lb/1.5 kg chuck steak,
cut in 2 in/5 cm cubes
1 large onion, sliced
2 bay leaves
1 sprig of thyme
3 tbs brandy
½ pt/300 ml red
burgundy
4 oz/120 g butter
1 oz/25 g flour
½ pt/300 ml stock
1 clove garlic
bouquet garni
4 oz/120 g salt pork or
streaky bacon, cut in
thin strips
24 small onions

This is a popular dish throughout France, one of
the standards of the French kitchen, often referred
to simply as boeuf bourguignon, or even just
bourguignon.

Put the meat in a large bowl with the onion, bay
leaves, thyme, brandy and wine and leave to
marinade for 3-4 hours.

Drain the meat and dry it, reserving the marinade.
Heat half the butter in a large pan and sauté the
meat until well browned on all sides — the
browning is important to the taste of the dish.

Sprinkle the flour over the meat, stirring and
shaking the pan so it amalgamates with the butter.
Pour over the strained marinade and enough stock

8 oz/250 g small
mushrooms
salt and pepper

Serves 6

just to cover the meat. Bring to the boil, stirring continuously, put in the garlic and bouquet garni and season with salt and pepper. Cover the pan tightly and transfer it to a preheated oven, 325°F, 160°C, gas 3 for 3-4 hours, until the beef is tender. Check occasionally to see if more stock is needed.

Heat the remaining butter and sauté the salt pork until it softens. Set it aside and brown the onions, then put them with the salt pork and sauté the mushrooms. Add the salt pork, onions and mushrooms to the pan and continue cooking in the oven for another 45 minutes. Remove the garlic and bouquet garni and serve.

The bourguignon can be kept for up to 2 days in the refrigerator and reheated gently before serving.

Gâteau de marrons
Chestnut dessert

1½ lb/750 g chestnuts
2 cloves
8 oz/250 g sugar
3 eggs
a few marrons glacés

Serves 6

Boil the chestnuts with the cloves, then peel and purée them in a vegetable mill. (If you prefer to omit this step you can use canned chestnut purée, with a little powdered clove added, but the taste will not be quite as good.) Beat together the sugar and egg yolks until pale and creamy, then stir in the chestnut purée. Beat the whites till they stand in peaks and fold them into the mixture.

Butter an ovenproof dish, such as a soufflé dish and pour in the mixture. Cook in a preheated oven, 300°F, 150°C, gas 2 for 45 minutes. When the dessert is cold sprinkle the top with small pieces of marrons glacés and serve with cream.

147

MENU 5

Ecrevisses à la nage

. . .

Lotte de rivière à la meunière

. . .

Clafoutis de pommes

Wine suggestion

Chablis

Ecrevisses à la nage
Crayfish in court-bouillon

24 live crayfish
1 small carrot
1 small onion
2 shallots
salt and pepper
bouquet garni
¾ pt/450 ml white
burgundy

Serves 4

Slice the vegetables thinly and put them in a pan with the bouquet garni, salt, pepper, wine and ½ pt/300 ml water. Simmer for 10 minutes or until the vegetables are cooked.

Bring the court-bouillon to the boil, plunge in the crayfish and simmer for 8-10 minutes. They are cooked when they are red all over. Heap the crayfish in a bowl, reduce the cooking liquid by half and pour over the crayfish.

Serve lukewarm.

Lotte de rivière à la meunière
Burbot meunière

4 burbot of about 8 oz/
250 g or 4 large fillets
¼ pt/150 ml milk
salt and pepper
1 oz/25 g flour
4 tbs oil
2 oz/50 g butter
juice of ½ lemon
1 tbs chopped fresh
tarragon

Serves 4

Soak the fish in the milk for 15 minutes, then dry it well. Coat it in flour that is well seasoned with salt and pepper.

Heat the oil and butter in a frying pan until very hot and cook the fish until golden brown on both sides — about 10 minutes for whole fish, 6-7 minutes for fillets.

Transfer the fish to a warm serving dish, sprinkle with lemon juice and tarragon and serve.

Clafoutis de pommes
Apple dessert

1 lb/500 g good eating
apples
4 tbs sugar
4 eggs
3 tbs flour
¼ pt/150 ml milk
butter
icing sugar

Serves 4

Peel, core and chop the apples and sprinkle with
the sugar. Beat the eggs, flour and milk together
and stir in the apples.

Butter a shallow ovenproof dish, pour in the
mixture and bake in a preheated oven, 350°F,
180°C, gas 4 for 30 minutes. Sprinkle thickly with
icing sugar and serve hot.

Glossary of Food Terms

Starters

charcuterie	cold meats (pork)
crudités	raw vegetables
escargots	snails
potage	soup
terrine	a type of coarse pâté

Meat (Viande)

agneau (gigot de)	lamb (leg of)
boeuf (filet de)	beef (fillet steak)
bleu	very rare
saignant	rare
à point	medium
bien cuit	well done
brochette	kebab
côte/côtelette	chop
entrecôte	steak (rib)
jambon	ham
lapin	rabbit
lièvre	hare
mouton	mutton
rillettes	potted pork
saucisse	sausage (fresh)
saucisson	sausage (dry)
veau	veal

Offal (Abats)

boudin	black pudding
cervelle	brains
foie	liver
langue	tongue
ris (de veau)	(veal) sweetbreads
rognon	kidney

Poultry (Volaille) and Game (Gibier)

caille	quail
canard/caneton	duck/duckling
coq	cockerel

faisan	pheasant
oie	goose
perdrix	partridge
pintade	guinea fowl
poulet	chicken
sanglier	wild boar

Fish (Poisson) and Shellfish (Crustacés/Coquillages)

alose	shad
anguilles (en gelée)	eels (jellied)
bouquet	prawn
brochet	pike
cabillaud	cod
coquilles St. Jacques	scallops
crevettes	prawns/shrimps
écrevisse	crayfish
fruits de mer	mixed shellfish
hareng	herring
homard	lobster
huitres	oyster
langoustine	scampi
lamproie	lamprey
lotte	monkfish
loup de mer	sea bass
maquereau	mackerel
moules	mussels
saumon	salmon
truite	trout

Vegetables (Légumes)

ail	garlic
artichaut	artichoke (globe)
asperge	asparagus
carotte	carrot
champignon	mushroom
chou	cabbage
choucroute	sauerkraut
choufleur	cauliflower
épinards	spinach
haricots verts	French beans
navet	turnip

oignon	onion
petits pois	peas
pomme de terre	potato
au four	baked, roast
purée	mashed
poireau	leek
poivron	green/red pepper
riz	rice

Fruit

ananas	pineapple
cassis	blackcurrant
cerise	cherry
citron	lemon
fraise	strawberry
framboise	raspberry
groseille	redcurrant
mûr	blackberry
pamplemousse	grapefruit
pêche	peach
poire	pear
pomme	apple
prune	plum

Recommended Reading

Economy and Society in Burgundy Since 1950, Robert Aldrich, Croom Helm, 1984

Through the French Canals, Philip Bristow, Navigator Publishing Ltd, 1970

The Golden Age, Joseph Calmette (1949), trs. Doreen Weightman, Weidenfeld & Nicholson, 1962

The Court of Burgundy, Otto Cartellieri, Routledge & Kegan Paul, 1929

Wines of Burgundy, Graham Chidgey, Century Pubs., 1984

The Works of Colette, Secker and Warburg, various editions

Phoenix Frustrated, the Lost Kingdom of Burgundy, Christopher Cope, Constable, 1986

Country Wines of Burgundy and Beaujolais, Patrick Delaforce, Lennard Pubs., 1987

Medieval Sculpture in France, Arthur Gardner, 1931

Burgundy, Landscape with Figures, Peter Gunn, Gollancz, 1976

Burgundy, Vines and Wines, Anthony Hanson, Faber, 1982

Great Wines of Burgundy, Duijker Hubrecht, (Trans. from Dutch) Mitchell Beazley, 1983

History, People and Places in Burgundy, Neil Lands, Spur Books, 1977

Armies of Medieval Burgundy, N. Michael, Osprey, 1983 (children's book)

Burgundy and the Morvan, Michelin Green Guide, Current edition

Barging into Burgundy, Gerard Morgan-Grenville, David & Charles, 1975

Burgundy, Robert Speight, Collins, 1975. Companion Guide

Dijon and the Valois Dukes of Burgundy, William Tyler, 1971

Philip the Bold, Richard Vaughan, Longmans, 1962

John the Fearless, Richard Vaughan, Longmans, 1970

Philip the Good, Apogee of Burgundy, Richard Vaughan, Longmans, 1970

Charles the Bold, Richard Vaughan, Longmans, 1973

The Wines of Burgundy, H.W. Yoxall, Penguin, 1974

Geographical Index

Index of Recipes

OTHER TITLES IN THIS SERIES

TRAVELS IN ALSACE & LORRAINE
TRAVELS IN BRITTANY
TRAVELS IN THE DORDOGNE
TRAVELS IN THE HOLY LAND
TRAVELS IN THE LOIRE
TRAVELS IN NORMANDY
TRAVELS IN PROVENCE
TRAVELS IN TUSCANY

All the titles offer the reader a ten/fourteen day journey through the region pointing out places of interest, hotels and restaurants, with special emphasis on the food and wines of the area. Each book also contains a mapped itinerary with distances and times for each day of the journey.

As well as hints and tips on what to buy and eat in the region, readers are provided with a selection of recipes and menus to enjoy on their return.

All titles now available from bookshops. In case of difficulty, please contact Merehurst Limited, Ferry House, 51-57 Lacy Road, Putney, London SW15 1PR, telephone 01-780 1177.